MAC...

It's All In Your Head

Asbjörn Torvol

BECOME A LIVING GOD

Copyright

Disclaimer

Personal success depends on work ethic, so results will vary. Consider all information adult knowledge and not legal or medical advice. Use this at your own risk. If any problems occur, contact a licensed psychologist or doctor immediately. The Publisher is not responsible for consequences of actions. This book is for readers of age 18 or older.

Credits

Author: Asbjörn Torvol

Artist: Gary Rosenberg

Editor: Timothy Donaghue

Publisher: Become A Living God

DEDICATION
Asbjörn Torvol

I DEDICATE this small tome to the greatest teachers, mentors and guides who have provided me not only with greatest of apprenticeships but with memories to cherish for a lifetime. In the path to Ascent our mentors are not only our greatest teachers, but our greatest friends and family.

To all the mentors who have guided me on my journey you have my greatest thanks and in my gratitude, I dedicate this tome to you: Dean Kirkland, Charles McBride, Li (aka E. Vasquez), Arron Burr and also William Allen Wheeler who passed away from cancer in 2016; May he rest in peace and may his legacy live on through us all.

FOREWORD
Edgar Kerval

THROUGHOUT time men have always been interested in changing the elements from within and the environment. Magick emerges as an important element in which the adept can mold their will in order to make the diverse elements change. Magick is the individual or collective art to cause a change internally and externally according the Will.

Magick is the art of transformation or transmutation into a sense of divine consciousness. One of the most important points of Magick is to liberate yourself from restrictive beliefs you were brought up with. Not to forget the interaction within the diverse gods/goddesses are acts of magick.

In few words, we can say that Magick is everywhere of each action in nature and its living beings exploring the will and the intent to do changes according to that will. Every inner quality forged manifests exponentially in the external world and the inner words; They are all acts of magick.

So, from these perspectives we also can say that Magick in essence is the use and control of natural energies and power of will to produce, to effect and cause needed change. There are three basic sources of natural energy or power used. Throughout this grimoire, you can go deep into the quintessence of man exploring the diverse forms of magick in different traditions.

It is worth to mentioning that a deep magickal power is in the deep of subconscious and through diverse methods of exploration we can access and develop it. Magick power is the force of death and life, the source of everything, the power of the universe and the void that created existence and nonexistence, form and unformed.

TABLET OF MAGICK

INTRODUCTION

THROUGHOUT my entire spiritual/occult journey I have delved into many areas of magick and I have path-worked many systems. Yet regardless of which system I have decided to path-work there has always been a similarity with all of them. A foundational base that seems to fit every tradition, every system. I like to use the house analogy to explain this. Every house is built with a foundation, every house is built with the same foundations and yet the way each house is decorated is unique and different.

Magick to me is no different. There is a foundation to all practices and some traditions have been this exact foundation on which the rest of my practice relies upon. At my core, I am a Norse Vitki (Shaman/Sorcerer) and yet the foundation for my work bleeds into several other areas of spirituality and magick forming the base for all that I do and work with.

This tome has been written with the intent to provide you with that foundation. When names, symbols and images are stripped away from magickal traditions and systems they can all look very similar, and in this we see the mechanics of how it all works, why it works and how to better work with it. This tome aims to break it all down for you, so that you can see the spiritual world we live in, with a much broader perspective and a deeper understanding of how to best utilize it.

Throughout this book, you will be exploring many areas of spiritual study as well as scientific relations to that study. Hermeticism, Thelema, Ceremonial Magick. Psychology, Energetic Sciences,

Hypnosis. This book will dissect the mechanics of magick and manifestation to provide you with the tools to refine and excel at whichever system you choose to practice. This will be a journey through my own life and the foundations that I have built, but also a pathworking into understand the nature of reality itself and where it is we sit within it.

In this journey, you will break down reality and peer upon its simple complexity. You will dive into the ocean of your sub-conscious mind to understand association of magick. Your perspective of magick will be challenged and much of what you will read may be uncomfortable. But I ask you to truly contemplate the text within these pages. As it was said by Aristotle:

> *It is the mark of an educated mind to be able to entertain a thought without accepting it.*

With this all in mind, I hope that this information will not only bring clarity and dispel the many misconceptions and romanticisms of magick but also provide you with new tools to further push you on the path to ascent. I wish you well with this pathworking.

Stay True & Stay Awesome.

—ASBJÖRN TORVOL

WHAT IS MAGICK?
Chapter 1

The Science and Art of causing Change to occur in conformity with Will. — Aleister Crowley

THE most common and widely accepted description on what magick is was written by Aleister Crowley in the context of Thelema. Thelema being a religion based on philosophical law by the name of Thelema. Aleister Crowley believed in the objective existence of magick. He chose to spell the word "Magick" with the letter "k" at the end to differentiate between "magic" (stage tricks and illusions) and "magick" as in his own description.

Throughout Crowley's life he gave several different definitions of magick the most common and popular being "The science and art of causing change to occur in conformity with will". However, he also said:

> *"Magick is getting into communication with individuals who exist on a higher plane than ours. Mysticism is the raising of oneself to their level."*

He saw Magick as a pathway between religion and science so much so that in his book "The Equinox" was given the subtitle of "The Method of Science; the Aim of Religion". In this book, he expressed a positive sentiment toward science and the scientific method, urging magicians to keep detailed logs of their magickal work. The hypothesis of this was that the more scientific the records were the better understanding the magician could draw from them.

What I love about Crowley and his work is that he did not see magick from the perspective that is was a past and primitive practice but rather believed it had to be adapted and tailored to suit the new age of science. This same concept is applied in all of my own work. I believe that while it is necessary for us to acknowledge history and the old ways of spirituality and magick, that at the end of the day we need to bring into the future as we grow, society grows, and technology grows. With this we do not just repeat history, but create it. We do not just learn the old ways but refine them and improve them. Many magickal practitioners want to practice ancient magicks but few want to invent newer and better ways to achieve those results, through learning more about the old and bringing them into the new.

BREAKING MISCONCEPTIONS

In Crowley's main definition of magick we can dismiss many of the misconceptions around magick. To quote for a great friend and colleague:

> I hold the belief that Magic is not 'Magical', that it does not 'just happen', nor is it 'miraculous'. — S. Ben Qayin

The first of these misconceptions is that Magick is an exclusive gift that certain people are born with. Now this extends not just to magick as a whole but to certain areas of magick. Psychics, Spiritual Vampirism, and much more. While some people can be born with a natural skill or talent I have never been one to accept its exclusiveness. I firmly believe that anyone can develop any technique, skill or connection with enough work and time.

Over all Magick is not an exclusive gift to certain individuals or certain bloodlines. Neither is magick mystical as many romanticized ideals would have you believe. It is not a skill you can achieve or an ability you can acquire. Magick itself is built into the very fabric of reality and your very essence. Simply put, Magick is the Mind; and as you work through this tome this will become more and more apparent.

Magick is one the underlying mechanics of life itself and even the most mundane of things are indeed "magickal" by this definition. Now in Crowley's descriptions of magick he suggests that magick is "action" and while this is true it is however slightly misleading. Magick is thought, emotion as well as action bleeding into every single thing that we do. In fact, everyone is performing magick and on a continuous basis, mostly unknowingly.

One of the many truths of magick is that you do not have to be aware of it, nor does it need to be intentional. In fact, the majority of magick is unintentional. The only difference between the magician/practitioner and everyone else is that the magician is aware of, involved with and in control of his or her magick. This then cuts away the second misconception and that is that magick is intent.

THE NATURE OF MAGICK

All magick I psychological in nature and at its core. Extensive rituals, magickal tools, exaggerated psychodrama does all have its place, however, it is not essential. The greatest magicians can perform magick at anytime and anywhere within his own mind. To quote from one of my own mentors:

Be very wary of anyone in this business who keeps telling you that you can be a master at magick if only you spend reams of cash on specialist equipment; in an emergency if you're down the pub with your mates and something comes up you can't say hang on a minute let me nip home and get my robes an athame. If you can't do magick dressed in only jeans, tee shirt and old trainers and armed with only a box of matches or a lighter you shouldn't be in this game. — Dean Kirkland

Every magician no matter how advanced is always using their own mind, psychologically to manifest result and change. This element of practice is so deep that it remains true even with practices such as evocation and possession. The deeper you go into this concept of mind, its responsibility, its impact and how it affects the conditions of reality you live in, the more this will become apparent.

With all of this in mind, pardon the pun, it does open up the next important principle for understanding the real magick.

SCIENTIFIC SPIRITUALITY

Science as a whole is one of the most important principles of magick. Not just in understanding the nature of energy but even to go as far as the nature of reality. It is not uncommon to find science and spirituality at war with each other, and this is because popular traditions, and fields of study tell us that it must be one or the other. We are told that it must be either science or spirituality. The reality could not be further from the truth.

Science and spirituality go hand in hand as it concerns real magick. It is often speculated that spirituality and magick have always been a head of science, and that science has been trying to catch up with it for years. When you combine science and spirituality, and let them complement each other and bounce off each other, you begin to debunk false information, fraudulent scams. Additionally, you create a potential to elevate yourself and your own experience of life as a whole. In this sense, the study and practice of magick is the study and practice of scientific spirituality. To put it simply, Magick is science through the eyes of spiritualism.

MIND OVER MATTER

It would seem pretty fair to say that magick is simply mind over matter. Although there is a quote that fits the basic starting point for understanding the nature of magick. That quote is:

Every thought is a prayer and every word is a spell.

With magicks connection to science we can conclude that magick itself has a set of principles that outline how it can be utilized. These principles while scientific in nature are found in the occult philosophy of Hermeticism (a philosophy based primarily upon writings attributed to Hermes Trismegistus). The Hermetic principles lay out the foundations for all of my magick work, including the mundane. Hermeticism as a philosophy I would say fits every single magickal system and current, and even without the deeper depths of magick such as evocation, possession, and working with spirits and gods, these principles can aid in just making mundane life much easier when applied.

This is where the rest of magical practice becomes apparent. As we understand these principles we can then look at where we need to invest our time. One of these obvious places is in psychology and human behavior. The key to real magickal practice lies within your own being, your own mind, and your ability to observe yourself and the reality you have created. As cliché as it may seem, know thyself.

ALL IS MIND

Chapter 2

THE ALL IS MIND; The Universe is Mental.
— *The Kybalion.*

WHEN it comes to the foundation of my own system there are two key principles. These two principles will be outlined in this chapter and the next two. On their own they form the most important concepts to magick, spirituality and path-working as a whole. These two principles alone allow the practitioner to dissect and understand any experience, ritual, or magickal formula. The first of these principles, is the principle of mind. As stated in the previous chapter all magick is psychological and as such we must start at the beginning... and the beginning of all things is mind.

THE LAW OF MENTALISM

In Hermeticism the first Principle of Seven is called the Law of Mentalism. This Law embodies the truth that all creation is a result and manifestation of mind. Now with this in mind, pardon the pun, we first have to nail down what exactly is meant by mind. If all is truly mind then that suggests the universe itself was created. Does this mean God? Not exactly. While many religious dogmas will tell you that "God" created everything, I prefer to see it from a much looser perspective. The universe itself is a living intelligent mind. It is created however what the creator may be is unknown, yet there is a theory.

Most of this theory will be understood more clearly in the next chapter however with mind alone we can outline creation. I want you to ponder for a second, where exactly do our thoughts come from? When we get an idea or more so a random thought, where exactly does that thought come from? Sometimes thoughts come from other thoughts. What we call train of thought. Yet even in that case, where exactly do our thoughts come from?

They come from silence, from darkness, from void. This is also the nature of our universe. As you understand the law of correspondence this will be more clear, but let's just say for argument sake that the universe exists within us and by understanding ourselves we understand the universe. The only difference is size. We are micro and it is macro and so the processes of the universe as it concerns creation is only difference in size rather than actual processes.

Thoughts come from nothingness, and since thoughts come from the void, that is where the universe comes from. It has been said that life itself is a dream and with this perspective it is easy to agree with it. The universe was created from nothing and by nothing. Since our thoughts are capable of coming from simply nothingness the universe itself is capable of doing the same thing.

So, with this theory in mind (and there are different variations of this theory) it becomes clear that every single thing that has happened is the result of a mental state which preceded it. For anything to exist, thought has to form first. Simply put, thoughts lead to the manifestation of things and events, creating our state of existence and quality; thus, reality itself is a result of thought both individually and collectively.

There is no single thing that exists apart from or outside of mind. This is where perspective comes into play. While perception is not truth, the perspective we have on things, events, and reality as a whole creates the reality that we experience. The perspective and focus we have, determines our reality. What we think about, be it consciously or sub-consciously affects our experienced reality. To quote from the bible (which when taken from a different perspective, ironically gives insight on magick and how it works):

According to your faith, so be it onto you. — Matthew 9:29

Now with this law over all it does suggest a potential paradox that needs to be nailed down early. If the All is mental, then we do not really exist and yet we all know that we do exist. Once the law of Vibration is explored this all comes together however we can go over a brief explanation. To keep it simple everything is made out of one thing, and that is energy. Energy exists in a constant state of vibration. Our minds decode that vibration information and we project an interpretation of that vibrational energy into a physical reality. This is how our corporeal world is created. As it has been said "reality is a dream".

THE MIND & MAGICK

With that bit of insight, it becomes clear that magick is simply "mind over matter". It is for this reason the mind is the most powerful tool of the magician. The mind is what allows us to perceive and experience reality. We can create our paradise with this tool, and yet we can also create the harshest hells for ourselves. The mind is always doing magick even when the practitioner is not consciously doing it. It is for these reasons that the magician has to be responsible for his or her mind.

Thoughts become things. If you see it in your mind, you will hold it in your hand. — Bob Proctor

Before we jump into manifesting through mind there is one other part of the concept to go over, and that is change. This law outlines to us perfectly the conditions to make change in our lives. If we want change to occur in our life it must first begin within our minds. Thought has to come first. This is one of the most basic principles of magick. Since all things begin with thought, all magick is then a result of thought; hence my conclusion of all magick being psychological in both nature and its core. This however, does not just apply to our intentional thoughts, but rather all thought. Our state of mind as a whole as well as the vibrations we are radiating will determine what will manifest in our lives. As Einstein said:

> *We cannot solve our problems with the same thinking we used when we created them.*

It is for this reason that the magician needs to be responsible for everything he or she creates by being responsible for everything he or she thinks. It requires the magician to monitor their thoughts on a constant basis until it becomes habitual.

One of the simplest of techniques in doing this is to tag each thought. If a negative thought comes to mind stop and say aloud or in your ahead I reject this thought. As this becomes habitual and natural the practitioner will begin not only to manifest more positivity in their life but will also begin to protect their own minds and reality from unnecessary negativity. This is the beginning of mental refinement and as such magickal refinement.

Our thoughts are so powerful that we can even be guilty of cursing ourselves. We tell ourselves negative things and those negative things manifest, as if by magick. Simply put if you project negativity it will come to you, and it will become because you yourself will have created it. Yet if you project positivity you will in turn create it. Now this does not just apply to your own thoughts but the things projected on you by others also. As much as people hate to admit this they have a choice to be affected by the thoughts and words of other people. There is a choice to reject negative projections from others. If someone offends us it is because we have chosen to let them. It is very easy to flick the switch between yes or no, and yet most don't because they are stubborn to it. If you want to change what's in your life you have to first change what's in your mind. To bring forth desire you must begin with it in the mind. To quote from the bible again:

> *All you need to say is simply 'Yes' or 'No'; anything beyond this comes from the evil one. — Matthew 5:37*

With this bible quote, many will automatically reject it because of its origin, and because their perspective does not allow them to accept it. Yet when you think of the "evil one" as the ego it all seems to make sense. See you don't have to react to other people's negativity… it's your ego that pushes you to do it; and you could easily by choice choose not to. Even at this point in the book many will be challenged in accepting this information just because of some of these quotes. Being able to move perspective to find insight is the mark of a true magician on the path of ascent.

THE TRIANGLE OF DIVINITY

Now typically this next concept is often broken down in a more scientific context and while I do love and appreciate that method I want to look at this from a Kabbalistic view. One of the main focuses of this tome is to challenge the magician/reader with potentially emotional based responses to information. Now while this seems like a hostile method of giving information the whole point of this is mind, and in order to truly free the mind for ascent the magician has to be able to entertain thought without accepting or rejecting at first emotional response; hence my deliberate use of biblical quotes to reference magickal concepts. As such for this concept we are going to look at the Triangle of divinity.

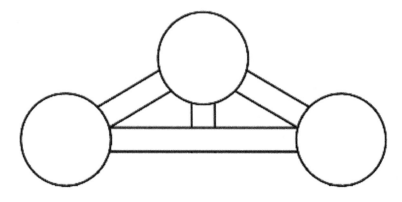

In the beginning was the Word, and the Word was with God,
and the Word was God. —John 1:1

The triangle of divinity is also known as the first triangle, the three supernals, the supernal triad and the holy trinity. In Kabbalah (a tradition of Jewish mysticism) the triangle of divinity is the three sephirot (emanations) at the top of the Kabbalistic tree of life. These three sephirah and the triangle as a whole are representative of both the head/mind of the human body, and the three aspects of divinity.

The triangle of divinity is comprised of three sephirot. Kether (Hebrew meaning "crown") which is placed just above the head. Chokmah (Hebrew meaning "wisdom") and Binah (Hebrew meaning "understanding" or "intelligence") which are placed at either side of the head.

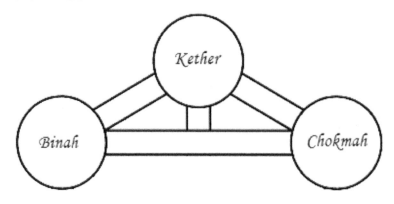

Glory be to the Father, and to the Son: and to the Holy Ghost.

The Kabbalistic tree of life as a whole has many correspondences, and so in looking at the triangle of divinity there is a lot we can take from it. However, we are going to keep this in the context of mind, perspective and how it mirrors the magickal formula of manifestation.

One of the most common correspondences of the triangle of divinity is the holy trinity itself. In Christianity, the holy trinity is comprised of the "father", "the son" and "the holy spirit" which refer to the three aspects of divinity. In Hinduism, this trinity is comprised of "Brahma", "Vishnu" and "Shiva". In Kabbalah, this trinity is comprised of Kether, Chokmah and Binah. Overall the triangle represents the three aspects of divinity, the divine itself and divine consciousness.

As above, so below, as within, so without, as the universe, so the soul.

The triangle of divinity is placed upon the head of man on the Kabbalistic tree of life. The placement of this triangle on the head is not placed there by mistake. We are divine and as such the triangle of divinity exists within our own body blueprint. As it is without so it is within. The human mind can be broken down into three parts. The conscious mind, the sub-conscious mind, and the collective unconscious (also called the divine consciousness).

These three parts can be placed onto the triangle of divinity in perfect correspondence. Our conscious mind corresponds with Binah, our sub-conscious with Chokmah, and our collective unconscious with Kether. This tells us a lot about our connection to the divine and to all knowledge. The path from Kether (top of the tree of life) to Malkuth (bottom of the tree of life), works its way down in a zig zag style direction. Kether connects to Chokmah, and then Chokmah to Binah. The key here is that Binah, our conscious mind, does not have a direct link to Kether which is the collective unconscious. However,

Chokmah which is our subconscious mind, does have a direct link to Kether.

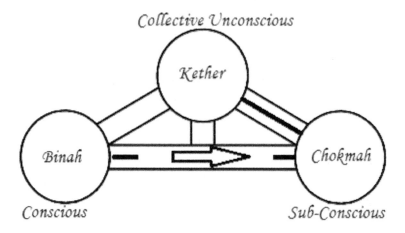

This tells us a lot about our magick and how it works. The magician uses his conscious mind (Binah), which is the masculine force, the fiery will, to make an impression upon the sub-conscious mind (Chokmah). The sub-conscious mind which is the feminine force, then takes that impression, the blueprint and gives birth to manifestation. The collective unconscious or the divine consciousness (Kether) is what provides the knowledge for the sub-conscious mind to manifest the initial impression. The important part to grasp here is that our conscious mind doesn't have a direct link to the divine, only our sub-conscious mind. Binah does not have a direct link with Kether in this specific instance. It is for this reason that the magician needs to establish proper communication with the two halves of his mind and bring a balance between his conscious and sub-conscious mind. Additionally, it is also important to bring balance to both halves of his physical brain which are also correspondent of these sephirot.

Another key insight here is that Binah is also representative of our ego. Our conscious mind which is where ego resides does not have a link to the collective unconscious/divine consciousness (Kether). While our ego does serve a purpose, it has to be controlled and in balance. The conscious mind and the sub-conscious mind must be working in unison. Binah is the masculine energy, the conceiver and Chokmah is the feminine which then gives birth to creation. If we are ruled by our ego, if our ego is in dominance then it lessens our power with magick and manifestation. Balancing Binah and Chokmah, both halves of our mind is the only way to attain proper control and power with our magick.

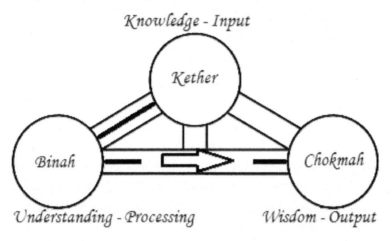

If we take the triangle away from the rest of the tree and look at it in and of itself we also see that it outlines human behavior. Kether which would be input or knowledge, which would travel to Binah in which that information would be processed or understood. Finally, the information would travel to Chokmah which would be the output or action. Input, processing and output, or knowledge, understanding and wisdom. It is the responsibility of the magician to make sure that this path is clear. The information taken in is of quality, as if quality goes in quality comes out. Additionally, this should be taken into consideration of magick and life itself. If negativity goes in it will come out and yet if positivity goes in it will come out; again, hitting on the importance of mind.

To the magician, the Triangle of Divinity is not only the understanding of being divine but also the understanding of how their mind and magick operates. All begins with the mind, all magick begins at

Kether. Additionally, all behavior begins first at Kether. On the Kabbalistic tree of life there are multiple paths of direction, but for magick itself, it always begins at Kether. This triangle represents is the archetypal world, the plane of will, spirit and divinity. Even outside of the Kabbalistic tree the science of this concept is simple to see. The process of magick and how it manifests is not too difficult to understand.

Our minds create thoughts, that travel to the subconscious mind and then manifest in our reality. This is the simple secret to manifestation. However, there still remains once question. If it is this simple, why do so many struggle with manifesting the result?

The answer to this is again not too difficult to understand. The biggest blockage of magick manifesting is our conscious mind and its filter. In psychology and hypnosis, the conscious mind is what filters information. If someone were to tell you a story and ask you to repeat it back to them straight away you would remember the majority of the detail. Yet if they were to ask you 2 hours later the majority of the detail would be forgotten as the longer information sits with the conscious mind, the more of it is filtered.

It is for this reason the magician needs to be able to set their intention, set their work, magick, ritual etc. and then be able to forget about it completely. For he who is certain need not think twice. In this when our conscious mind lets go of that thought, the sub-conscious takes over. If a ritual, intention, magick is done the longer it sits in the mind the longer it will filter and dilute for, this is how our magickal power gets diluted. We have to get the conscious mind out of the way in order for the result to manifest.

This is why when practitioners are desperate for a result it takes longer, as their conscious mind is constantly worrying and as such thinking about it. Additionally, it is for this reason when we are looking for something we do not always find it. How many people look for love their entire life and then when they stop looking it finally turns up? Because that is magick and it follows the same process. The mundane is magick which I cannot stress enough.

With this in mind there is a solution for the overly conscious minded folks out there who struggle to set it and forget it. Every time you go to do a ritual, intention or magickal work write down five things to do afterward that will take 100% of your conscious attention to do. Rock climbing, art, reading, writing to name a few. It has to be something that requires your conscious attention at all times. This way your conscious mind stops thinking about the magick and that will allow the sub-conscious to take over and manifest the result.

LASHTAL: THE THELEMIC MAGICK FORMULA

The word "LASHTAL" is often considered as a Thelemic formula of magick. Similar to the Triangle of Divinity it contains certain corresponds to the concepts of mind and self-divinity adding to the solidity of our magickal formula. LASHTAL can be divided into three parts, LA, SHT and AL.

The first part (LA) means "not", and the last part (AL) means God. Additionally, LA can also mean "naught" and AL can mean "two". The middle or central part (SHT) means "to wander". One implication or understanding of LASHTAL is "not to wander from God". This can be interpreted as not to wander too far with the ego as it will pull us away from the self-divinity and ascent. Not to forget that it also can refer to forgetting our individuality and following the collective dogma. However, there are other perspectives and interpretations.

It implies both the singleness of purpose and selflessness, to the magician there is another strong implication here. We are God, and the law of correspondence tells us this which we will be exploring shortly. With that in mind, it is clear that the further you wander from the self (your inner self, your inner god), the less power your magick will have. Simply put "do not wander too far from your true self".

When broken down into its three parts LASHTAL creates the triangle of divinity. LA meaning "not" or "Naught" is the nothingness, the source in which all things emerge. It is the mind, Kether, the father. Overall it is simply non-being. AL meaning "Two" is being, it is the destination of creation, it is manifestation. SHT is the processing. The process to creation or the becoming of things. This process works in both directions. From the Nothingness (LA), comes creation (AL), and from creation (AL) when it dies it returns to nothingness (LA). Additionally, AL is also correspondent with Malkuth. LA is the crown, the divine, the source, and AL is the kingdom in which creation is manifested. SHT is what happens in between, the process or road in which creation travels upon. In a simple definition, LASHTAL is Non-being, becoming and Being. Not so difficult to see its outline of the process of magick, life and creation.

THE INDIVIDUAL
Chapter Three

I N my entire career as an author, public figure and magician there is one single thing I have emphasized more than anything else. That one thing, is the individual. Espousing perspectivism over dogma and absolutism has been one of my sole focuses and it has not ever shifted.

This comes in two main forms. The first is that embracing who you are as an individual is the only true way to ascent, freedom and over all power. This has become so important that even my own slogan was formed around it. Stay True & Stay Awesome is a direct reference to this concept. The second comes down to the nature of magick itself. Since magick is manifested through each individual's sub-conscious mind all magick, ritual and ceremony is subject to the association of the individuals own mind.

For example, let's take a dog as a stimulus for the mind. There are two people, Person A and Person B. Person A grew up around dogs, and as such reacts positively to the dog stimulus. Person B however, was bitten and traumatized by a dog when they were young and as such reacts negatively toward the dog stimulus. Simply put, two people can react completely differently to the same stimuli. Colors, sigils, sounds, smells, tastes, all of the five senses included.

Magick falls under this same psychological principle. All magickal symbolism and indeed all symbolism because all is magick, relies upon the individual rather than the collective. Even ritual, ever symbol, every magickal tool needs to be tailored to the individual's sub-conscious needs, and so copying by rote, word by word will not always produce the greatest of results. It is for this reason that we say Know Thyself. Know thyself in this instance is not a reference to know who you are, but rather understand how your mind relates to stimuli.

By understanding your own associations to stimulus, you can understand how to best create and modify ritual to get the results you need. This is just basic psychology. All rituals are subject to the subconscious and so any grimoire you read, ever ritual, every spell is but a template for you to add your own associations to achieve the result.

This goes for interpreting gods, what kinds of things to give in offerings, which incenses to use, colors etc. Once you understand your mind, you will better understand your own magickal needs. This is but another reason why the law of mentalism is so important to the magicians pathworking.

THE LAW OF THELEMA

Do what thou wilt shall be the whole of the Law. Love is the law, love under will. — *The Law of Thelema*

The law of Thelema or as I like to call it scientific illuminism, embodies the concept that all beings and each individual possesses a "True Will". This is a single overall motivation and purpose for each individual's existence. It is each individual's innermost true nature and grand destiny in life. In order for any being to attain fulfilment and freedom they need to follow their own "True Will". This is but another reason why the need for self-exploration is of such great importance.

Again, the stress on knowing thyself. Following this will means acting and operating in perfect harmony with one's own true nature. Simply discovering and acknowledging it is not enough, one has to act in harmony with it in order to attain fulfilment. Hitting back on mentalism again our thoughts and actions have to be in unison with each other.

The main task of all individuals is to discover their "True Will" and then follow it with appropriate action. This will however does not spring from conscious intent, but rather interplays between the deepest self and the entire universe. It needs to be understood that this Law does not mean to do whatever you want, but rather to stay true to yourself and not to push toward something that you're not or can't be.

Every man and every woman is a star. — *Aleister Crowley*

Each individual is unique and has their own path and purpose in the universe. For this reason, every "True Will" is different and because each individual has their own unique perception of the universe, no one can determine the "True Will" of another person. It is the responsibility of each individual to discover it for themselves. In order for anyone to be one with their "True Will" they have to eliminate any false desires, conflicts and habits which are not in alignment with their "True Will". It means acting in alignment without a resistance or push. Like a leaf on a stream simply flowing with the current.

Love is the law, love under will.

The nature of the Law of Thelema is that of love. Each individual must first unite themselves with their true nature, "True Will" or true self, in love. Love has to come before will, as stated "love under will". This is not a reference to romantic love but rather the expansive force of consciousness. Only through this expansive force (love), can anyone truly come to higher states of consciousness. This is why it is important to love yourself. As cliché as this may seem, unless you love, embrace and accept your own individuality you will be a slave to the collective.

This type of love is also known as agape, unconditional love or spiritual love. The Thelemic Law "Do what thou wilt shall be the whole of the law," must remain in context of "Love is the law, love under will". This means that any act of will must be performed with love of your own individual self. (higher consciousness). To add to this, it also a reference to the principle of nature law, called the principle of care. If you do not care/love what you are doing, then what you are doing will not bare good fruit. This care is putting the right attention and focus onto what you are doing. At its foundation, as only action based in this love/care can result in alignment with "True Will" and yield the results desired. This is another important part of the journey to ascent.

THE OBEAH & THE WANGA

Also the mantras and spells; the obeah and the wanga; the work of the wand and the work of the sword; these he shall learn and teach. — AL I:37

This next individual based concept was taught to me by my former mentor William Allen Wheeler, who sadly passed away in 2016 from cancer. He was a Thelemic Practitioner and as such many of the Thelemic concepts in this tome were passed onto me from him. It is because of him that my stress on the individual is so strong. The next Thelemic concept is another very important one again hitting back on the law of mentalism.

The terms Obeah and Wanga are African diasporic words that are used in the sacred texts of Thelema. Obeah comes from West African Igbo sources and has a close relation to hoodoo. A Wanga is a magickal charm found in the folk magick of Haiti and thus is connected to Vodoun. In the sacred texts of Thelema these terms were not meant as a literal reference to Obeah or Wanga but rather a symbolic and philosophical concept. Obeah is meant in reference to actions, while Wanga is in reference to words. Obeah and Wanga together is the entirety of external expression.

Magick is the management of all we say and do.
— Aleister Crowley

This Thelemic concept is in essence very simple. Act as you say and say as you do. Both action and thought must be in alignment. It is very easy to say, think and believe in something and yet have your actions be in contradiction with that. Your "Obeah" which is your actions must be in alignment with you "Wanga" which is your thoughts and words. Both have to be in correspondence with each other. It is the responsibility of the magician to align his Obeah and Wanga, as the following of our "True Will" is dependent upon it. Magick first begins in the mind, and as such our actions must mirror those thoughts and spoken words.

This concept also relates to how ritual magick should be conducted. The ritual space while seemingly outside of you is within you. A magician must treat ritual space as an extension of himself and his mind. This concept in its totality is the alignment of mind, body and soul and their extensions. Thoughts, words, beliefs, actions, worldview, ritual. The inner space must all be in alignment with each other. When the inner space is in conflict, when things are not in alignment the magician does not have fullest amount of power.

THE DANGER OF DOGMA

It is not difficult to see why the individual is so important to nail down early on in magickal exploration and practice. There is a danger to dogma as it concerns the path to ascent. First however let's nail down what I mean by dogma.

Dogma definition: a principle or set of principles laid down by an authority as incontrovertibly true.

To us as occultists this definition is adapted slightly more loosely and from a slightly different perspective, and to this concept both are valid. Dogma in both these instances, is any form of religious or spiritual absolutism. When information on a spiritual topic is made absolute. For example, if someone were to state that this particular ritual to manifest this result has to use this exact single tool. That would be an absolutism, and as we have already established, all ritual ingredients and components are subject to the subconscious. With this in mind it is clear to see why dogma is illogical and dangerous for the magician to adhere to. For this reason, we have to always bring things back to the individual needs and not the collective absolutes.

Even with "spiritual mythologies, gods etc." they still remain open to interpretation. Mythology itself is created by man, documented by man and as such will always be subject to interpretation. Perspectivism. Everything is perspective. Fact and spiritual insight do not always line up together perfectly. While a mythology may state something as a fact, the spiritual insight of that to the individual may be ever so slightly different. To touch on my own magickal tradition as an example, many think that Baldur (Norse God) is dead because he dies in the mythology and yet many including myself has spiritually worked with him. IT depends on the individual's perspective. The Key here is to base your spiritual truths on what you experience and what you associate sub-consciously over what is written down and set in stone.

CORRESPONDENCE
Chapter 4

N EXT to the Law of Mentalism and mind the second most important concept in the foundation of the magicians magick. Just like the rest of my foundation this goes straight back to Hermeticism.

> *As above, so below; as below, so above. — The Kybalion*

This law of correspondence embodies the concept that which is "above" is like to that which is "below", and that which is "below" is like to that which is "above. The "above" is a reference to the macrocosm, the very large or the totality, while the "below" is a reference to the microcosm, the small or the individual. At its core this law tells us that the macrocosm, the seemingly outside/external world is but a reflection of our inner world/self. They are reflections of each other that cannot be separated. Just as each individual exists within the all, the all also exists within each individual.

> *Man know thyself; then thou shalt know the universe and God.*
> *— Pythagoras*

Since the macrocosm and the microcosm are reflections of each other and exist within each other, it becomes clear why self-exploration is so important. If you are to learn the secrets of the universe and the divine, you need but only look within. This is one of the most important concepts for all magicians to grasp. The universe exists within you, and you are indeed divine as we have already nailed down. To know the workings of the individual is to know the workings of the universe and to know the workings of the universe is to know the workings of the individual. There are no degrees of separation between you and the universe. The only degrees of separation exist within the mind. It is at this concept, that we really do go down deep into the rabbit hole.

First clean the inside of the cup and of the dish, so that the outside of it may become clean also. — Matthew 23:26

There is a direct correspondence between the way we think and feel on the inside, and the way we act and experience on the outside. Our experience of reality is a reflection of ourselves. It mirrors, corresponds with what we have on the inside; again, going back to the law of mentalism which goes hand in hand with this law. The reality we experience on the outside is really what's going on inside of us. It is for this reason that being in alignment with what you desire is so important. If you want to change your life on the outside you must first change what's on the inside.

I am God. So it's easy to play him. They say God is in all things. So if God is in me, then I am in God. Therefore, I am God. God does not exist without me. — Morgan Freeman

You do not have to look up to the sky to call upon the divine. The same forces that keep the planets in motion also keep the atoms in your body and the environment in constant motion. When it comes to ritual this is one of the most fundamental concepts when it concerns direction of intent. It takes a lot longer for your intention to travel out into the far universe than it does to the universe that is within you. There is a lot less distance to travel. As said there are no degrees of separation, the separation only exists within the mind.

PATHWORKING ASCENT – KETHER & MALKUTH

He had a dream, and behold, a ladder was set on the earth with its top reaching to heaven. — *Genesis 28:12*

Since the Kabbalistic tree of life has so many correspondences there is no point in trying to place a universal concept on each piece. As much as it is the tree of life it is also the tree of correspondence as each piece holds many concepts and truths, just like one picture holds a thousand words. In Kabbalah, it is said that the path from Malkuth (Hebrew for "Kingdom"), all the way up to Kether through the other Sephirot is the way to the divine. This is called the ladder of the divine, the ladder to god, or sometimes the ladder of ascension. This directional path from the kingdom to the crown, is what the many call pathworking to Ascent, or The Path to Godhood. The magician's path begins in the physical, corporeal realm and his/her aim is to elevate themselves, be it for ascension, to reach god, or simply to higher states of consciousness. To the magician this path is the journey he/she is seeking to walk.

But seek first His kingdom and His righteousness, and all these things will be added to you. — *Matthew 6:33*

Kether and Malkuth are also points on the movement of magick. All magick begins first in the mind, all things first exist in thought. Thus, all things exist first in Kether. Kether is the starting point for all things. When magick manifests, when thoughts become creation they end in Malkuth. What started as a thought in Kether has become a manifestation in Malkuth the physical realm. Additionally, when something dies or is destroyed it starts that process at Malkuth and returns back to Kether. Thus, it is fairly easy to see how these two sephirot work together are correspond.

Another correspondence of these two sephirot is of the law of correspondence itself. As within, so without. The inner world of the self, our mind, our thoughts, our inner space is Kether. The outer world, our experience of reality is Malkuth. What we think about we bring about, thus Kether and Malkuth in this correspondence mirror each other. What the inner self projects such as thoughts, emotion, state of being, will be mirrored in the outer or external experience. By looking at how things are in your external world (Malkuth), you can come to understand how things are like in your inner world (Kether), and vice versa. Additionally, with the law of correspondence in mind, Kether exists within Malkuth, and Malkuth exists within Kether.

SAMATHA & VIPASSANA

It wouldn't be the greatest of tomes without throwing in some actual techniques and practices to go with these concepts. With this in mind the simplest techniques to start working and applying these principles is some Buddhist meditations.

Do not dwell in the past, do not dream of the future, concentrate the mind on the present moment. — Buddha

In Buddhism, there are two different types of meditation. The first is Samatha and the other is Vipassana. Samatha here means concentration and Vipassana means insight or experiential knowledge of bodily and mental phenomena. The purpose of Samatha meditation is to attain higher levels of concentration, focus and peaceful living. The purpose of Vipassana meditation is to attain a deep concentration of the mind and also to liberate the self from mental and physical suffering (known in Buddhism as Dukkah). This liberation is done through realization of our body-mind process and their true nature. Going back to the law of mentalism this is simply working to condition our own minds.

Since Samatha meditation is practiced to attain higher concentration of the mind, it stands as almost as a method of mental training.

The idea is to concentrate your mind on a single object of meditation. A common method of Samatha practiced often by magicians is to place a point around one inch in size on the wall at eye level. The idea in this method is to keep your eyes fixed on the point and keep your focus and concentration on the point. Another and more common method of this is the focus on the breathing. The breathing in this meditation is the object of meditation. The key in these meditations is condition the mind and its focus. If the mind wanders, gently bring it back, and with time, repetition and practice your concentration will develop.

Sit in a posture that is comfortable. Straighten your back and keep it erect. Relax your shoulders and keep your head evenly balanced but tuck your chin slightly inwards. Let your tongue touch the palate. Relax your face and close your eyes. Focus your mind on the rising and falling of breath. Bring attention to the small space between your upper lip and the nostrils. Feel every breath in and out. If the mind wanders, gently bring the focus back to the breath.

With a decent level of concentration, you will be able to realize mental and physical phenomena as they really are, and with this you can do away with all kind of mental impurities, defilements, paradigms and more. With Vipassana the practitioner can begin to clean his mind and begin to shape it into a more beneficial state. Vipassana is also a great method of grounding the self.

Vipassana is done by first going into a Samatha meditation, typically a focus on the breath. Anything else that draws your attention away from your breathing such as sounds, smells, thoughts, emotions etc. are "secondary objects". If a secondary object draws your attention away from the breathing you should focus on it for a moment or two. While focusing on the secondary object for that moment you want to give it a label such as "Thinking", "Memory", "Hearing", "Desiring", "Feelings" etc. This is called "noting".

Noting is simply making a mental note which identifies something in general but not in detail. When you are drawn away by a sound, instead of labelling it with what the sound might have been, or what you thought it might have been, simply label it "hearing". The key is to label it with a general term or word, almost as if you were categorizing it, rather than defining it or identifying it. Once the "secondary object" has been labelled/noted move the focus back to the primary object (breathing).

The point here is to observe the secondary objects, be aware of them without attachment. Being able to let thoughts and sensations arise and pass of their own accord. Noting or labelling is the method of preventing you from being carried away, and keeping your mind aware but unattached. With practice, you can develop clear seeing, inner peace and freedom in relation to those objects as you are no longer mentally carried away by attachment. Additionally, you begin to develop a stronger connection with your mind, condition your mind and shape it into a more beneficial state.

THE NATURE OF OUR GODS

With the law of mentalism and the law of correspondence nail down, the rabbit hole gets much deeper. If the all is mental, and all that is within is also without and vice versa that tells us some big insights on our gods as well as any other entities such as demons, angels, spirits, etc.

All of these beings we work with magickally exist both within our minds as well as outside of us as external forces. Every god, every demon, every angel etc. are just as much psychological personifications as they are external forces and forces of nature. This is a huge insight into much of the ritual work that we do. These two concepts, mind and correspondence take us so deep into magick and we haven't even touched on the rest of these principles yet.

Evocation and possession are just as psychological, and internal as they are calling forth from outside of us. Additionally, when we project magick outward we are also pulling in at the same time.

VIBRATION
Chapter 5

Nothing rests; everything moves; everything vibrates.
— The Kybalion

WITH Mind and Correspondence understood and implemented the next foundation to be placed is looking at the makeup of reality itself. It is at this point we go deeper into energetic science and the Law of Vibration.

The Law of Vibration embodies the concept that there is no such thing as rest, as dead or non-motion and that everything is constantly in motion. There is no such thing as true or absolute rest and as such if something is in existence then it is in motion. Nowhere in the universe does there exist something that is at complete rest. At the most fundamental level, the universe and everything which comprises it (including people, thoughts, words, emotions etc.) is at its core, pure vibratory energy manifesting itself in different ways. This includes not only the seen but the unseen also.

The first principles of the universe are atoms and empty space...
the atoms are unlimited in size and number, and they are borne
along in the whole universe in a vortex, and thereby generate all
composite things—-fire, water, air, earth. For even these are con-
glomerations of given atoms. — Democritus

To really understand this law, it is essential to understand one thing. Everything is energy, and science through quantum physics has shown us this. Everything in the universe is vibrating at a frequency, different things having different frequencies. In this sense, we are living in an energetic sea which we call the universe and we are all connected through that one thing (energy). Everything has its own frequency and all of it is governed by the law of vibration.

Death in this sense is an illusion because true death would the cessation of all motion and energy, and as stated nothing is ever at rest. As such the universe has no true solidity. The matter which makes up all things, is merely energy in a state of vibration. While things may seem solid, they are actually comprised of millions and millions of particles which are vibrating and creating the illusion of solidity. Through the law of vibration, we see that all reality on every level, be it physically, mentally, spiritually is simply energy and vibration. All things are connection but this same energetic fabric differentiating only by degrees of vibration frequency.

Do not be deceived, God is not mocked; for whatever a man sows, this he will also reap. — Galatians 6:7

This law tells us some very important things to our life and our magick. Energy and its frequencies operate with something called resonance. If two things share an identical frequency they will attract each other. Simply put, "like" attracts "like". Every energy will attract other energies that synchronize in frequency. Since words, thoughts, emotions, states of being etc. are all energy, what you project you will attract. This is very similar to but also slightly different to the law of Karma, what you put out has a huge potential to return to you. You reap what you sow. If you project negativity, negativity will be drawn to you. This is an important rule of magick we have already concluded.

It is for this very reason that baneful magick is not looked kindly by many. Now while I have no issue with it myself, I do recognize that in doing it the practitioner is also affected. Three-fold, Four-Fold and Seven-Fold laws are subscription based and do not scientifically nor logically synchronize with this concept. None the less when we push out our magick it will have an effect on us. This does not mean baneful magick should not be practiced, but rather acknowledged that in doing it, it will affect you. Even the native America shamans have a similar concept in that, in killing another you kill a part of yourself in the process. Energetically this is vibrational syncing with what you project. This applies to the mundane also.

> *Everything is energy and that's all there is to it. Match the frequency of the reality you want and you cannot help but get that reality. It can be no other way. This is not philosophy. This is physics.* — *Albert Einstein*

Magick at its core is the use and manipulation of energy and its frequencies. The law of vibration outlines a good base on how magick actually works. This is commonly known as vibration synchronicity or vibration magnetism. The all begins with the mind. This is why it is so important for the magician to be in control of his or her self. We are all constantly projecting energy in what we say, what we think, what we feel. We are responsible for the things that come into our lives. Thus, the magician projects what he wants to attract. To really come to control your own magick, you must first come to control what you are projecting. Project good vibrations and it will return to you. Project negative vibrations and they too will return to you.

By this point you will be starting to see how all of these concepts intermingle with each other and bleed into each other. Like a tapestry, you only begin to see the picture when you put more of the pieces together.

THE NATURE OF REALITY

To understand the great mystery of magick it is paramount to understand the nature of reality itself. Energy and vibration as a whole is the single most important part of magick and it lays down the entire base for all magickal work. Like magick, Reality in its simplest form is energy in states of vibration. It is the literal building blocks of every single thing in existence. To look at it from the most simplistic view reality is only a frequency in which we do not detect directly to in its base form but rather interpret and form into three-dimensional reality based on our own minds, both individually and collectively. In this sense if the mind is the magick machine then energy is the fuel that allows it to operate.

Reality that we experience is the energetic frequencies that we have decoded. Like a radio our minds tune into to the certain frequencies and project that into a three-dimensional reality. In many ways, our universe is much alike a virtual reality. Three-dimensional reality is an illusion.

If you break down and look at an atom, the majority of that atom is empty space. It has no solidity; how can you create a solid world out of something that is not solid. The answer is simple, it is not solid. Now to the magician this makes life seem like a lie, just a fake illusion. In fact, even I had this same challenge. We believe that because the physical is an illusion and to many a prison (hence the heightened desire for spirituality), many seem to think this devalues their magick. I disagree entirely. I would say that because reality is this pliable we can create the existence we want; it is because of this illusion that ascension itself is possible.

> *We are perceivers, we are awareness; we are not objects; we have no solidity. We are boundless ... We, or rather our reason, forget this and thus we entrap the totality of ourselves in a vicious circle from which we rarely emerge in our lifetime.*

We create a world, a reality from the energetic frequencies of the universe that functions just like a virtual reality only more sophisticated. We take the vibrational information and decode it into a reality that appears to be real but is just illusion. All the time we are decoding this reality in this apparently solid state. It is possible to draw a 2D picture in a certain way that the brain decodes it as three dimensional. This is tricking the mind and since the mind is decoding all the time you can manipulate it to decode in a certain way. Again, I stress the importance of mentalism.

Now because Magick itself is intertwined with energy, it becomes apparent at how we are able to use magick in these seemingly magickal ways. We draw a sigil on a piece of paper and burn it on a candle, and a few days later we experience the manifestation of that intent. Simplified we are projecting energy, changing it, altering it, to bring that result to us. To make this as simplistic as possible, all magick is simply energy work.

The more we understand these concepts the more we see magick isn't as mystical as many would believe. The magician is only decoding reality in a different way when used to do certain things. In chaos magick this concept is known as meta-belief. Being able to change perspective and in turn synch with different frequencies to achieve a required result.

However, with the law of mentalism and vibration together is tells us that reality exists within the mind. Add correspondence in that and we understand reality is both created by the individual and the collective. It is for this very reason that no religion, spirituality, or tradition is wrong but at the same time none of them are right. The idea of a single true way is simply wrong and the only "right" or "true" way is individual based.

To take the afterlife as an example, those who believe strongly in heaven will creating that reality and the same goes for any other belief, be it hell, Valhalla, Nirvana, etc. This energetic possibility is limitless and no person is bound to a finite rule of manifestation. There does exist all possibility and the limits are simply self-made, be that a conscious limit or a sub-conscious one.

There is no such thing as miracles, there is only understanding reality and the magick more than you are when you perceive them as miracles. A person can walk through fire in one state of consciousness and not get burnt yet in another state of consciousness can end up in hospital within minutes. It is just simply your connection to what you are interacting with. Your interaction with reality that is the difference. If you believe strongly enough that you will get burnt then you will because you will create the energetic reality of that. But if you go to another state beyond that then you could very well not get burnt. All you are doing is decoding it in a different way and we have the power to program ourselves a paradise. This is the key to magickal breakthrough.

> *What is real? How do you define real? If you're talking about what you can feel, what you can smell, taste and see, the "real" is simply electrical signals interpreted by your brain.*

HOLOGRAPHIC UNIVERSE

If you take a holographic print and cut in half, you don't get half of the hologram, but rather a half-sized version of the whole print. It is just a smaller version of the whole thing, and as such as above so below; again, touching on correspondence. We are holographic in nature, we are the all, we are the universe, we are everything, but just as a smaller version, and so everything is just a smaller version of the whole. Now as bold as that statement may be I like to take it from a slightly different angle. The all simply exists within. Every person holds the all within themselves. Every cell in the body carries the whole universe within it. The human energy field mirrors that of the earth's energy field. As above so below. Just as we have chakra points in the body, the earth too has chakra points as does the rest of the universe.

We are in essence living in this holographic universe and magick is somewhat like the holographic internet. If you understand what we call the internet in the way we use it on our computers we begin to see a very similar relation.

The only place the internet exists in the form that we perceive it, is on the computer screen. Websites, graphics, colors, texts and documents etc. All that is only on the computer screen. It only exists in that form on the screen. Everywhere else it is just electrical circuits and signals along with the mathematics etc. This is the same with television, the only place it exists as we perceive it is on the screen. And like the internet it exists everywhere else only as a frequency field. Reality is not different. This holographic internet we exist in is just energetic information and we decode that information and what we decode and how we decode decides what our experienced reality is. Exactly as our computers create images, texts, etc. from data. It is another example of the reality illusion.

The biological body is essentially the computer that taps into the holographic internet of reality. We are decoding it mostly unknowingly into the reality we think is real and universal. Like real computers if manipulated and programmed it can firewall off certain things so that the user can only access that which suits the one controlling it. We can decode huge and vast amounts of this holographic internet but the majority of it is being firewalled off just like the computers we use at home.

If the doors of perception were cleansed, everything would appear to man as it is - infinite.

Magick is the energetic sea. Frequency is everything because everything is a frequency as we have already established. We live in the energetic sea of magick and its vibrational information in which we decode into this illusory reality. There is not empty space between everything they are only different projections and expressions of this energetic sea. We decode it into a reality which is a projection and expression. As such if you want to affect all the fish in the sea at the same time you affect the sea. If you want to affect all beings at the same time you need to affect this energy sea.

It is because of the nature of our reality that there are no bounds to what we can do. If you want to change something that seems impossible all you have to do is remove that limitation from the mind and decode the information that changes that reality. Now admittedly this is easier said than done but the theory itself is sound. Simply put magick is everywhere and in everything, it is energy and energy can be manipulated.

If you want to walk through fire without getting burnt you need to simply decode reality in that way. If you want to make things move with thought you need only decode reality in that way. However, if you tell yourself it cannot be done, it's impossible and you place the mental limitations in stone in your mind, all you are doing is decoding a reality where you cannot do these things. We have the universe in the palms of our hands and yet we limit what we can do with it. We have the ability to create for ourselves the greatest of things.

THE BIOLOGICAL INTERFACE

Every one of us is not our body but rather our consciousness. We live in a shell a vehicle which is the body to interact with this reality. If you want to go on the internet you need a conduit; an interface in which you can access that collective reality. We can all access the world-wide web but we need a computer to access it.

Our consciousness is doing that same thing but only more sophisticated. It takes on the biological computer so to speak which is the body as its interface and its immediate energy field which is the mind. The mind allows us to interact with this reality. Mind operates through thought and that is a low level of perception. Consciousness operates on something called knowing. It is all knowing, it has all knowledge. It is all, has been and ever will be and therefore it doesn't need to try and work things out, which is why in a state of consciousness one is in a state of silence. When you get stuck in mind and interacting with the mind it chatters all the time, whereas if you are in consciousness it's silent. To touch back on our scientific break down of the mind, our conscious is comprised of all three aspects of "mind". Conscious, Sub-conscious and Collective unconscious in perfect unison.

We live in a world of things and everything seems to be things. This is not the prime reality we think it is. The prime reality is consciousness, silence. It doesn't have to work things out because it knows. Many think silence is nothing. Yet everything comes from that silence and goes back to the silence. Consciousness at its highest level is all possibility and in that silence, is all possibility. Another reason why meditation is so important to the practicing magician.

When one starts to talk, they pull through sound one possibility out of all possibility which then through the senses becomes one possibility. When one starts to talk, noise comes from silence and when one stops talking it goes back to silence. This is why the importance of nothingness and oneness is important in our practice.

The Tao is like a well: used but never used up. It is like the eternal void: Filled with infinite possibilities.
— Tao-Te-Ching, Verse 4

This is the same for space. What is space? Space is nothing and yet it defines a lot of things. A container without space is not really that useful. This reality here is things and yet what defines things is also nothing. In this reality of things, things come out of nothing and then go back to nothing. A person is born into the world of nothing and once they pass they go back to nothing.

VIBRATIONAL MAGNETISM – SYNCHRONICITY

One of the benefits to having a higher state of awareness is being able to witness vibrational magnetism or what the magician refers to as synchronicity; seemingly random and coincidental events that really aren't random or coincidental at all. Now hitting again back on the law of mentalism and correspondence, stimulus is relative. To quote from the Vikings TV series,

When you hear thunder you hear thunder,
but when I hear thunder I still hear Thor.

Synchronicity itself still relies on the sub-conscious association of the individual. When any given ritual is done the result and or conformation always comes through this synchronicity. This is because of vibrational magnetism.

There will have been a time where you will have asked yourself a question, and you will have either stumbled across the answer later or it'll just pop into their head and you'll just know the answer. Typically when that happens within hours or days they will come across something that will confirm that answer. And this is part of how this magnetism operates.

Nothing happens by chance.

Manifestation happens as a result of one's intentions and state of being regardless of if it was intentional or not. It happens for everyone but it's just that the practitioner is constantly aware of it. It is the way in which someone's energy is going to manifest. Things don't just spontaneously appear suddenly in front of them. The way that a result of your intentions and energy comes into life is through that of synchronicity. If you had an intention to get more money, seemingly random coincidental events would happen that would bring you more money. And it would seem like a normal part of life but except for the fact that you know you had the intention to get that to happen. This is because of vibrational magnetism. When you have that intention, which is a frequency and other frequencies that relate will attach and be pulled into your life. This is yet another key piece in understanding the machine of magick.

Now the time it can take to actually manifest can differ. Even if you didn't practice using intention you should still be aware of synchronicity, as people are always making intentions and putting out energy whether they know it or not. It's important to look at the things that are coming into your life. Look back every so often see if you can trace it back to something that was said or done either by you or someone else.

It is very easy for another person to influence another's life through what is said and read even just picked up by the sub-conscious mind. This is why it is important to seal the mind and guard the gates of the mind. If you're not controlling your energy and your magick someone else will be. Once you start to become aware of these synchronicities and vibrational magnetism as a whole and not to forget the way these things come into one's life you can start to be able to foresee it. In many ways, this is one of the first principles of divination.

This is what is meant by being the center of your own universe. When you are in your circle, you are the center of the universe because you are orchestrating it all. Synchronicity now serves the practitioner. But synchronicity as a whole is simply what is happening not the how or why it's happening; for that we need to fold in mentalism, correspondence and intention as a whole.

The state of being of each person is also partially responsible for what comes into that person's life. State of being is again a frequency as is everything. When you're in a state of being a state of mind whatever that may be, the frequency that is put out will draw in other frequencies that relate. Being aware of your frequencies, state of being and mind as well as intentions will make it easier to control what comes into your life, if your frequency is relating to something you don't want coming in, it is your responsibility not anyone else's. To quote from earlier, "like attracts like".

Vibrational Magnetism and synchronicity doesn't care about what you see as good or bad, if you put out a frequency, a thought or intention, that frequency is going to draw in those things into your life. It is the simple law of attraction. Every thought is a frequency and the more you think of that thought the more consistent that frequency becomes and the stronger that frequency becomes. If you think about something you don't want you're still putting out that frequency and those things will be drawn to you. You have to understand you are the magnet and you attract that in which you put out. Put out a frequency of illness and you will end up ill. Put out a frequency of love and you will end up with love. What you focus on becomes frequency and that frequency does not reject but draw into your life. This is my understanding of the quote "it is meant to be."

THE GREAT I AM

Now if focusing on what we don't want will still bring it to us, this concept now opens up a new insight. If we act as if we already have what we want, if we act as if it is already here, then that in turn will manifest it. This is what is known as the I AM. In order for us to ascend part of that is acting and performing as if we have already achieved that. In order for us to be rich we must act as if we already are. In order for us to have love we must act is if we already have it. This is how frequency is put out.

When you approach the Gods, Spirits, Demons etc. asking for aid, you must perform that ritual as if you are certain. To perform that ritual not as a request but rather a thank you. This is the magician's certainty. He who has no doubt, he who is certain need not think twice.

This is important for two main reasons. The first is that by doing this we aid in getting our conscious mind out of the way for the magick itself to manifest. Being able to do a ritual and then simply finish and move on will yield much greater and more consistent results.

The second is that the confidence this has, removed all doubt in our minds. Again, playing into the law of mentalism. By acting as if we are we begin to push that frequency out and in turn the likeness will attract the desire.

In addition to this, this is the establishment of Godhood. To not path-work to Godhood but to rather embrace the God or Divine that already exists within yourself. Remember that the only degrees of separation exist within the mind.

ENERGY WORK

Chapter 6

N OW if there is one thing to take from last chapter and I am sure you will read over it several times to get it all down. I am not ignorant to the fact a lot of that information is a lot to take in. For the sake of this chapter we are going to focus on the simple principle that all magick is energy work.

Energy work as a whole is so important that there have been books, courses, authors dedicated to that topic as a whole. There is so much possibility for energy work that to cover it all would take a thousand books like this. So, with that in mind in this chapter we are going to do something more practical. Outlined in this chapter will be several techniques to introduce you to energy work and how you can begin to interact, refine, and make use of it; intentionally of course.

Before we jump into that though there are some important details to re-affirm before we do that. The first is that mundane actions are energy work. When we wake up in the morning we immediately start the energy work. Walking to the store is energy work, picking up your coffee to sip from the cup is energy work. This is magick because magick is mundane. So, with these techniques bear in mind that mundane methods can be just as much a benefit as more ritualistic ones.

Just as a quick example, if you wanted to push out emotional energy, going for an intense run outside can do this. How? Well when we run we use up energy and with being emotional that emotional energy can be pushed out. Other methods of this as it concerns emotions would be holding a talisman and pushing mentally the energy out. There are hundreds of methods.

Your emotions are energy and as such can be implemented into magick to create results. In fact, I recommend using all emotion in ritual work. Use the current emotion to synchronize with what you are doing. If you are feeling emotionally successful do a success ritual. Push that emotional energy into perhaps a green candle. If you are feely angry perhaps channel it into destroying a part of your situation you dislike. For example, let's say I'm broke, out cash. I could use that anger in a ritual to destroy poverty. See this links right back to mind and perspective; of course, not forgetting to set and forget.

SUN-GAZING

Sun-gazing is the practice of looking directly into the sun. Since the human eye is very sensitive and the suns light can be damaging to the eye, the practice of Sun-gazing is done as the sun is setting or rising. The practice entails looking at the rising or setting sun with your bare feet on the ground, one time per day only during the safe hours. No harm will come to your eyes during the morning and evening safe hours. The safe hours are anytime within 1-hour window after sunrise or anytime within the 1-hr window before sunset. The length of time one should sun-gaze is up to the practitioner however a general rule is, if your eyes start to hurt stop.

There are many benefits to Sun-gazing, some spiritual, some physical. Physically, improved health, increased energy, clear thinking, and increased awareness are some of the common physical benefits. Spiritually the benefits are grounding the self and empowering the self. Additionally, fulfilment is commonly reported with sun-gazing. The practice of sun-gazing is also beneficial for the pineal gland.

*The images are manifested to man, but the light in them remains
concealed in the image of the light of the father. He will become
manifested, but his image will remain concealed by the light.*
— *The Gospel of Thomas 83*

Magically sun-gazing has an interesting concept. In the genesis story light is an important concept. When looking at this verse in Genesis we can see the symbolic truth. It outlines creation and how the magician is a creator. Before existence things were without form and void. This is symbolic to the nothingness, the unformed idea. Let there be light is symbolic to manifestation. God in this sense is the magician. As above so below, the magician is God. The sun is a powerful source of energy and all magick is energy work and manipulation. When sun-gazing, the magician absorbs the suns energy. This practice is but a physical, spiritual aid but also a meditation. It is symbolically connecting to the divine self, and drawing in energy of the divine. With the many benefits to health, mind and magick, it is also the affirmation of self-divinity.

*In the beginning, God created the heavens and the earth. The
earth was without form and void, and darkness was over the face
of the deep. And the Spirit of God was hovering over the face of
the waters. And God said, "Let there be light," and there was
light.* — *Genesis 1:1 – 1:3*

TEMPLE OF THE BODY

*Or do you not know that your body is a temple of the Holy Spirit
who is in you, whom you have from God.*
— *Corinthians 6:19*

We established pretty early on in that the magician's path is that of the mind, and that perspective is everything. Not only this but correspondences are woven into our very fabrics, and that everything is energy. With these three basic concepts in mind, a proper diet seems necessary. While the all is indeed mind that doesn't dismiss the fact that what you consume is what you will produce. Very simply food, drink and other consumables are energy, and if we consume energies that are not good for our body physically, then it won't be mentally or spiritually either. It has been said in many sources that the body is a temple. Your body is a "temple of the Holy Spirit". The Holy Spirit in this verse is a reference to your true self. "Whom you have from God". God in this is reference to your divinity. Very simply put the body is the temple for your true self and your divinity. You are a god and as such you must care for your body temple.

> *Make yourself strong Fortify your temple. Solidify your temple,*
> *and your empire will rise around you. —*
> *E.A Koetting in Conversations with Azazel*

What is within your body will in turn be projected outside of your body. As within so without. Even basic things like consumption have to be taken into consideration by the magician. Everything is energy and that adheres to the law of correspondence. If you want a healthy life you must first have a healthy self not to forget a healthy mind also. You need to bring that into yourself first. This is not to say the magician can only eat and drink healthy, but understanding accumulation is important. If more unhealthy energy is coming in than healthy energy then the unhealthy is what's going to reflect more dominantly. Moderation is key. It is the magician's responsibility to know and manage his intake. What goes in must come out.

The important thing to remember is that magickal work requires mind, body, and spirit. As such it is important that they are healthy and operating with the maximum power. The mind, body and spirit are the most important tools the magician has and diet is not just a practice of health but of respect for these important tools. With health comes strength, but also efficiency in how your body and mind operates. This is not just a physical practice but a psychological one also.

THE SACRED OM

But Om is something divine.
—Aitareya Aranyaka 23.6

In Hinduism "Om" or "Aum" is a sacred sound, considered to be the greatest of all mantras (a sound or word repeated in meditation). The syllable is comprised of three sounds, a-u-m. Om is said to embody the essence of the universe. In Indian philosophical belief, god created sound and the universe arose from it. Om is the root of the universe and all that exists within it. To the magician this is yet another correspondence. It is said that every word is a prayer and every word a spell. Words are sounds, sounds are vibrations. In the beginning, there is the word. It is easy to see this base correspondence.

The Om is the sacred sound, the divine vibration. As within so without, as without so within. When using the Om, you are energetically aligning yourself to the universe itself and your divinity. The Om is not just a sacred sound but a potent power word. The vibration of the universe and the sacred sound of the self. The magician makes use of the Om in these ways but also as a way to center and balance himself/herself. To bring the self into harmony with the macrocosm in an even flow.

To the magician, this is another example of how the law of vibration is key and Om is a simple foundation for touching the essence of this law. Everything is energy and vibration. Sounds are vibrations. As such when using the Om mantra, you are connecting with the energy of the universe and creation itself. You are connecting with the deepest levels of your soul. Allowing your body and mind to synchronize with this energy is to tap into the very source of all energy and all existence. Connecting with divinity on its most basic energetic level.

The simplest method for using this would be to sit in a basic meditation and vibrate the Om. However, this method opens up a new ingredient for our magickal practice. We now understand the importance of sound, and as such we can begin to use this same technique but with different vibrations. In my case as a Norse Shaman I will vibrate the names of the runes in this same method to energetically pull and push certain currents. This can be done with the names of gods, deities, and even just the simplicity of words as intentions.

Now let's take this energy work a little step further into a more physically challenging form. While vibrating tones, meditating and gazing at objects to absorb energies is good and in many way essentially to the practice of the magician it is important to find more active means of working with energy. Now it is at this point I could jump strait into Ceremonial Magick and while I do love that, I want to take this from a more eastern perspective/practice.

QIGONG

All ritual magick is a form of more physical energy work. With this in mind it makes sense that the magician conditions his own energy, as well as learn to manipulate it. Qigong or Chi Kung, is a holistic system of body posture, movement, breathing and meditation. Its benefits extend to mind, body, and spirit. Qigong is practiced cultivating and balance Qi (Life energy). To the magician, Qigong is another invaluable practice for the work of magick and self-development. As within so without, as without so within. If our energy on the inside is in bad shape then the energy we project into our magick will be the same. It is our responsibility to balance our inner energy and condition our control over our system. Additionally, the practice of Qigong develops the techniques for moving energy, which in ritual is an essential part of the process.

Qigong has many benefits. It strengthens the body physically, and acts as a great form of physical exercise. With the balance of energy in the body it aids in healing. Many practitioners claim that Qigong has aided in getting rid of illnesses quicker. Additionally, it aids in emotional balance, mental balance and allows the practitioner to access higher levels of awareness. Most importantly the practitioner learns how to control his own energetic self and how to circulate energy efficiently.

When it comes to ritual the accumulation of energy is important. At the very core, all ritual is energy work. If the magician's energy is blocked, imbalanced and not circulating properly, the ritual is going to manifest the same results. Correspondence and energy is key, not to mention the mental energy which also needs to be balance. It is the responsibility of the magician to balance and keep his system in good shape and Qigong does this in both the physical and the spiritual.

One of the many reasons why Qigong style techniques is important is because of our own energetic body and its state. Qigong is but one example of such exercises but there are many other techniques for working with the energetic system. Grounding is a big one. To take from my previous book "Ramblings of an Apprentice Vitki" the first grounding technique is done with the Goddess Jord, and aims directly at balancing the energetic system.

The simplest form of grounding is just to go outside with your shoes off and stand in the same spot for 20 minutes. Feel the energy come up one leg naturally then down the other. Naturally this will ground and balance the energetic system.

THE ENERGETIC BODY – CHAKRIC SYSTEM

Without going too far astray with the energetic system I just want to cover the very basics of the energetic body. To almost every single spiritual practitioner this is called the Chakra System. Energy and vibration while simply in and of itself extends into many areas for the magician to recognize. One of these areas is to understand his or her energetic system.

The chakras (energy points or nodes) are the main points of the energetic body. Each chakra is responsible for different parts of the body and as such if something is not working correctly in the body, it can be traced back to one of these chakra points. As such in knowing and understanding these points, you can take control over your energetic system and keep it in quality condition. These chakras are described as spinning wheels of light. There are seven major chakra points on the energetic body.

THE CROWN

Sahasrara or the crown chakra is pure consciousness/soul. This chakra is located at the crown of the head or just above it. It is represented either by the color purple or white. This chakra is related to one's spiritual connection to the universe, the ability to be open to all, and an overall cosmic understanding. This is the highest vibrating chakra and is considered the closest link to the soul. Not to mention the pinnacle of divinity itself, relating to Kether. With perspective, as a whole, interpretations of each chakra can differ slightly.

THE THIRD EYE

Ajna, or the third eye chakra is the higher mental self. This chakra is located between the eyebrows. It is represented either by the color violet/indigo or white. This chakra is the seat of intuition, awareness, and inner vision. This chakra relates to our ability to visualize and process mental concepts. How we "see" the world is determined by the state of this chakra. Mentally, this chakra deals with visual consciousness. Emotionally, it deals with clarity on an intuitive level. Additionally, this chakra is also linked to the pineal gland.

THE THROAT

Vishuddah or the throat chakra is mental self, communication, and expression. This chakra is located at the throat. It is represented by the color blue/light blue. This chakra relates to our ability to take

personal responsibility for our actions. Personal responsibility, creativity, communication, expression, logic, and reason are all related to
this chakra. Physically this chakra governs communication, emotionally it governs independence, mentally it governs fluent thought, and
spiritually, it governs a sense of security.

THE HEART

Anahta or the heart chakra is the point of feeling or the heart mind.
This Chakra is located between the breasts. It is represented by the
color green. This chakra gives us the ability to express love for ourselves and others. It is also related to compassion and intuitiveness. It
is through this chakra, we develop relationships and connections. Additionally, this chakra is responsible for the emotional self and unconditional love. Physically this chakra governs circulation, emotionally
it governs unconditional love for the self and others, mentally it governs passion, and spiritually it governs devotion.

SOLAR PLEXUS

Manipura or the solar plexus/navel chakra is the astral self. This
chakra is located behind the solar plexus. It is represented by the color
yellow. This chakra gives us a sense of our personal power in the
world. It also relates to destiny, psychic ability, determination, asser-
tion, personal power, and purpose. The solar plexus chakra is what
gives us the grounded and secure feeling of "I am". Physically, this
chakra governs digestion, mentally it governs personal power, emotionally it governs expansiveness, and spiritually, all matters of
growth.

THE SACRAL

Svadhishthana or the sacral chakra the etheric self. This chakra is located just beneath the navel. It is represented by the color orange.

This chakra relates to the quantity of sexual energy and vitality, security, creativity, and sincerity. This chakra governs reproduction, mentally it governs creativity, emotionally it governs joy, and spiritually it governs enthusiasm.

THE ROOT

Muladhara or the root chakra is the physical self. This chakra is located at the very base of the spine. It is represented by the color red. It is linked to survival instincts, a good self-image, and our ability to ground ourselves in the physical world. This chakra is the slowest vibrating chakra of the seven major ones. Physically this chakra governs sexuality, mentally it governs stability, emotionally it governs sensuality, and spiritually it governs a sense of security.

THE LEAD INTO CEREMONY

With the Three main principles (Mind, Correspondence & Vibration) down it is from here that the real magickal work can begin. While there are several other principles that bleed further into these three now the magician can lead into Ceremonial Magick and the principles not as deep into the rabbit hole as the former three.

CEREMONY
Chapter 7

I T is at this stage in the process where the best in me comes out. I am a huge lover of ceremonial magick and with the insight from previous principles I imagine you will be able to see the processes of ceremonial magick much clearer. The psychodrama will be understood much more clearly and the templates will be much more easily picked up by the practitioner.

However, before we jump into the overall templates for the ceremonial aspects of practice outlining some basic rituals and their uses. Now with the new knowledge you now have from the previous chapters do not hesitate to tweak the rituals you are about to do. Perspective is everything and as we know, all rituals must be tailored to the individual. This chapter is where you get to put your new knowledge to the test.

THE KABBALISTIC CROSS RITUAL

This ritual utilizes the archetypal symbol of the cross, which possesses deep significance in magickal work. The cross itself is a basic map, representing the circular horizon, the four quarters, four cardinal directions and also extends into deeper Symbolism such as the four elements. The purpose of this ritual is to expand the magician's sphere of consciousness, and to affirm one's unity with the divine.

In this ritual you will visualize a cross of brilliant light shining bright within your body. This cross symbolizes the intersection of the two primal dimensions. The vertical line which is the dimension of being, and the horizontal line which is the dimension of action. The vertical line of being, is visualized emanating from a sphere of brilliant white light floating just above the crown of your head (Kether). It will move down through your body, and enter another sphere of light encircling your feet (Malkuth). This forms the connection between the Source of All, and here the plane of manifestation or the material plane.

This visualization of the line of power running vertically through your body is a symbolic ritualistic expression of the individual connection between the upper and lower worlds. Through performing this ritual, you form a conscious connection with higher spiritual energies.

The horizontal line of action is visualized as a line of brilliant light running from a sphere of red light at your right shoulder symbolizing Geburah (Strength). The top of your heart center into a sphere of blue light at your left shoulder symbolizing Chesed (Mercy). The line is a symbolic expression of the truth that you are a conscious being with the power to make decisions. The red Geburah sphere at your right shoulder symbolizes your ability to make limiting decisions. The blue Chesed sphere at your left shoulder symbolizes your ability to make expansive decisions.

Geburah is also called Judgement and Chesed is called Mercy or Loving Kindness, and through forming a line between them that intersects with the vertical line of being at the center of your chest, you are symbolically placing yourself at the point of perfect balance and de-polarization. Where your decisions will be neither too harsh nor too lenient. You also symbolically locate your decisions at the point where they will be most greatly influenced by the higher spiritual forces flowing down from above.

This ritual is in essence a method of affirming that you know exactly where you are spiritually and what you are going to decide to do. This is the perfect metaphysical position, the magical high ground.

PERFORMING THE RITUAL

Begin by standing facing toward the East, the direction of the rising sun. Visualize a glowing sphere of white light, forming above the top of your head. Take time for this image to form clearly in your imagination and allow your thoughts to consider that this sphere symbolizes the source of all creation. Raise your right hand, place the tips of your fingers into this sphere of light, pull the light downward and touch your forehead, vibrating the word "Ateh" (pronounced, ahtah). This Hebrew word means "Thou art".

Slowly move your right hand down from your forehead and let it hover a few inches away from your chest. Visualize the light moving down with your hand, and that it continues straight down through your body till it reaches your feet. Try to visualize your body as semitransparent and that you can see the line of light moving down through yourself. Visualize another sphere of white light forming around your feet. Touch your chest with your right hand, and say the word "Malkuth" (pronounced mahl-koot). This Hebrew word means "The Kingdom," and the sphere at your feet symbolizes the here and now in which you reside, now perceived as filled with the light of the Divine. Allow this image to become clear and strong, and let your thoughts consider that you are the bridge between the Upper and Lower planes, and that it is through your decision that the Divine Light manifests. Place both hands at your sides while visualizing the upright line of the Cross.

Now raise your left hand and let it hover a few inches away from your right shoulder. Visualize a sphere of burning red light, forming around and within your right shoulder. Allow this image to become strong and clear. The red Geburah sphere symbolizes your power & vitality, your ability to define boundaries and defend them, your strength to resist harmful negative influences. With this in mind, touch your left hand to your right shoulder and say the words "ve Geburah," (pronounced Vih-G'boo-rah) which are Hebrew for "the Power."

Still keeping your left hand on your right shoulder, lift your right hand and let it hover a few inches away from your left shoulder. Visualize that a line of light is streaming from the red sphere on your right into your left shoulder where a sphere of glowing blue light forms, around and within your left shoulder. Allow this image to become clear and distinct in your mind, touch your left shoulder with your right hand, and say the words "ve Gedullah," (pronounced Vih-Geh-doo-lah) which, in Hebrew, mean "the Glory." The blue sphere symbolizes your ability to be giving, loving, compassionate, and forgiving.

While keeping your hands crossed over your chest, visualize the horizontal line of light moving through your chest, connecting the red and blue spheres and intersecting with the vertical line of the Cross right in the center of your chest. The horizontal line represents the complete spectrum of your moral/ethical actions, and wherever your consciousness falls on this line will determine whether your decisions are made for the sake of your Self or Others, and whether they are harsh or loving. At the point where the two lines intersect, visualize a glowing sphere of yellowish-golden light forming. This symbolizes Tiphereth, the central sephirot of Enlightened Consciousness that perfectly balances influences from above and below. Visualize the Tiphereth sphere moving downward slightly until it is at the same level as your heart now forming the base of a triangle with the Geburah and Gedullah spheres. See this clearly and vividly in your mind, and watch as its light radiates from within you to surround you and illuminate the room in which you stand. Say the Hebrew words "la olam," (pronounced Lih-Oh-Lahm) which are variously translated as "unto all the ages" or "forever."

Conclude by clasping your hands together, as in prayer, and holding them against your chest at the place where the sphere of golden light manifests. Say the word "Amen" (pronounced Ah-mehn). This expresses your conscious decision to elevate and shift your consciousness to a center of perfect spiritual balance.

Stand for a while and visualize the light of the cross glowing brightly within you. See the light radiate around you like a protective sphere, a circle of spiritual protection and illumination. Meditate on the symbolic significance of the ritual.

THE CEREMONIAL TEMPLATE

Now with the Kabbalistic Cross as a small starting ritual to get into the feel of ceremonial magick it's now time to take a dive into the templates of ceremonial magick as a whole.

The point of Ceremonial Magick as it concerns our previous principles is to use psychodrama (tools, complex names and steps, candles, robes, carbs, movements etc.) to make a bigger impression upon the sub-conscious mind. Now while these rituals can achieve the result without all that psychodrama it does help with over all immersion, thus helping with better results.

Anytime a tool is used that isn't just the mind in a ritual you are entering ceremonial territory. Every ritual in most cases uses this same formula from ceremonial magick. The Key to success with it, is to make sure every piece of the psychodrama is in perfect association and correspondence with the sub-conscious mind.

Anytime you look at a ritual you must tailor every single component to your individual needs and associations. By doing this you will have mastered the art of Ceremony. Every tool must add to the intent, purpose and goal and never steer away from it. Intuition is a great tool for figuring this out. It is because of this knowing thyself is of upmost importance and in all ways, be it knowing the mind and yourself as a whole.

With the Template of Ceremony nailed down, it is time to add the rest of the principles of magick and Hermeticism. With this it will provide you with the perfect formula for not just understanding magick but performing it to the best of your ability.

BALANCE
Chapter 8

I T is pretty common to find the term balance popping up everywhere in the occult. The concept alone has created been deeply
romanticized and yet it there is some important truths to it all.
Not so much in balance but in the Law of Polarity as a whole.

THE LAW OF POLARITY

The Law of Polarity embodies the concept that all things are dual.
Dark and light, up and down, left and right, negative, and positive,
etc. This law states that these things are the same in nature but different in degree. They are poles on the same concept. Duality itself is
inescapable and each thing has a positive and negative charge to it.
We cannot escape duality as it is built into the fabric of reality. These
seemingly opposite things are not actually separate at all. These things
are one in the same. Everything is dual, everything has poles and everything has its equal opposite, these things are identical in nature but
different in degree.

Polarity is displayed throughout many paths and in many ways.
Boaz and Jachin, the pillars of severity and mercy, yin and yang are
just a few of those displays. To the magician, Polarity is while a truth,
the realization of perception. Right and Wrong, good, and bad are
but perspectives. The Goal of the magician should be to maintain a
balance in all things, to never steer to one end or the other but rather

be one with the flow of polarity itself embracing both as necessary components of the web of reality. This is often called walking the middle path. The point of this is not only to maintain balance but to embrace natural duality. We all have light and dark within and to neglect one is to be unbalanced. Just as death is natural part of life, life to is a natural part of death and this duality is one of those natural cycles that we tend to cling to. As much as we want order we must also embrace chaos. It is for this reason that the true magician is not truly left or right hand path as it concerns magick but rather uses both through necessity instead of bias.

We will never be able to escape duality nor can we remove ourselves from it but embracing it in its wholeness without leaning to extremes is a virtue many do not possess. Balance prevents the magician for bias but also bring us closer to the nature of reality itself. Magick itself has this duality and embracing it benefits the magician in many ways. Polarity is like the terminals on a battery, positive and negative, if I take one of them away the flow of electricity stops. Therefore, I need this equal and opposite force because without there can be no movement. This is the same as the human body, that electricity is our life force and we need these terminals for it to move and flow. Polarization is the framework on the web of reality, as well as the main principle tool of practitioner. With one hand, we give and the other we take.

Many of the truths we cling to greatly depend upon our point of view.

What may seem right for one person might not be right for another. This world and the way society has been manipulated falls greatly on polarity. It has been very easy for those in the know to manipulate society through polarity for profit. If you look to things such as politics or religion this manipulation is very noticeable. People are manipulated into choosing a side and it has to be this side or the other side. The reality of it is that a Satanist can be just as extreme as some of the Christians they are claiming to be rebelling against. They are both identical in nature but different in their degree.

As stated it has become very easy to manipulate those people who are polarized. More often than not all a person needs to do is make a statement to a large enough audience and a war among them breaks out. The same person who created the statement profits from one of those "sides" whose focus turns to supporting the statement. For example, a food company might say something for gay marriage, the battle breaks out and the opposing side boycotts the company but everyone for it ends up walking through their doors to order their food. So even if the people have been split into opposing sides one can still profit.

Polarized people are easily moved and it is as simple as creating an opposing side to move them, either by repulsion or attraction. This is why it is important to de-polarize and become not so easily moved. To walk the middle path or middle pillar as some refer it to. It is about de-polarization and to bring balance to these two seemingly opposite sides. Reach a state where you're not for one or the other but stand in the middle and understand both degrees of the subject's nature. In this state of being it is a lot harder to manipulate or control that person however that person will find they have trouble relating to those who are polarized.

The polarized will have trouble relating to the other side, the de-polarized will have trouble relating to either of them.

Now even if a person walks the middle path/pillar and becomes de-polarized they still cannot completely remove themselves from duality. Without duality, this reality would not work. If I take one pillar of the human tree of life away the whole thing would collapse. So, in this reality both degrees are needed. Each degree of duality is like terminals on a battery. I need the positive and negative terminals to get the flow of electricity and without it the flow of electricity stops.

We need this difference in degree as without it there can be no movement.

This is no different in the biological interface. The electricity is our life force and we need the terminals for it to move and flow through. Polarity is the framework on that tree of life. We need the terminals, the pillars for the great electric flow of life and it is needed to complete the circuit. The aim of the middle pillar/path is to become grounded and de-polarized. To stand in the center and not lean toward one degree or the other. To sit in neutrality and work in neutrality. Being de-polarized gives one a deeper understanding of the degree in nature. The de-polarized can bring balance between the poles and bind them into one unique state. Everything begins with the work of the mind be it the consciousness or "the mind". Understanding the perspective of the mind is key. If you start with a polarized through, that which follows will be polarized. However, start from a neutral thought, that which follows will be balanced. When one starts to get into the habit of this, things don't become good experiences or bad experiences. They just become experiences.

THE JOURNEY TO THE MIDDLE PILLAR

For the sake of traditionalism and to test your own self with the knowledge provided in this tome you are now going to work up to the Middle Pillar ritual. The point of that ritual from this formals perspective is to aid in the de-polarization of self.

In ceremonial magick as a tradition there are two rituals to be learned and performed before doing the middle pillar. Now while many Black Magicians will reject these rituals because of emotional based responses to their own perspective I ask you to consider the perspective of these rituals. As you call upon the Divine and the Angels do not see them as external divine and angelic forces but rather the internal aspects and personifications of those entities. Perspective is indeed everything.

LESSER BANISHING RITUAL OF THE PENTAGRAM

Before performing this ritual traditionally, the Kabbalistic Cross ritual we did earlier is performed first.

Face east. Stretch out right hand pointing with index finger or athame (ritual dagger) and trace a banishing earth pentagram in visualized white light. "Stab it with your finger or the athame" in the center, and Vibrate: YOD HEH VAV HEH.

Turn south, with hand and finger/athame still extended while visualizing a line of white light, then trace another pentagram of white light and stab it in the center, and vibrate: AH DOH NAI.

Turn west, with hand and finger/athame still extended and visualizing a line of white light, trace another pentagram of light, and stab it, and vibrate: EH HEH YEH.

Turn north, with hand and finger/athame still extended and repeat drawing the circle and pentagram, stab it, and vibrate: AH GE LAH.

Return to face east, extend both arms to form a cross, and say: Before me Raphael, behind be Gabriel, on my right-hand Michael, on my left hand Auriel, for before me flames the Pentagram, and Behind me the Six-rayed Star.

Repeat the Kabbalistic Cross.

With this ritual as a whole I propose you to tweak it to your individual. Take the template of this banishing ritual and come up with your own method. Let this be the first ritual you create yourself (with banishing in mind of course), with the new knowledge this book has provided you with.

MODIFIED LBRP

To give you a little more inspiration and more of an idea of how these rituals can be modified here is an example of the Lesser Banishing Ritual of the Pentagram re-written and modified by Astrid Fallon's in light of this work, create with the intention of tailoring it to their individual needs.

Pentagram of Death (Modified Name): The association for his ritual is more of a hostile approach to banishing. By pushing out death energy/intent by default it kills any energy in the area that is not wanted, which in turn forms the banishing. Now this method is completely different than the original as it concerns intent, but this form does not work for me personally, however as we keep saying, it must work for each individual and in this case the student has indeed gotten the desired result.

Performing the ritual:

1. Place the blade/athame on your forehead, and vibrate the word Fatum Fati (Utterance, Oracle, Fate, Destiny, Life, Doom, Death, Calamity)

2. Place the blade on your mid-chest, and vibrate the words Mors Mortis (Death, Corps, Annihilation)

3. Place the blade on your right shoulder and vibrate the words Letum Leti (Death, Ruin, Annihilation, Death and Destruction)

4. Place the Athame on your left shoulder and vibrate the words Funeris Funus (Burial, Funeral, Funeral Rites, Ruin, Corpse, Death)

5. Clasping the Athame in your hands upon your mid-chest and vibrate the words Nex Necis (Death, Murder) So be it!

6. Facing the East pointing the Athame straight ahead make a pentagram vibrate the words Exitium Exiti (Destruction, Ruin, Death, Mischief)

7. Facing the South pointing the Athame straight ahead make a pentagram vibrate the words Occido Occidere Occidi Occisus (Kill, Murder, Slaughter, Slay, Cut, Knock Down, Weary, Death, Ruin)

8. Facing the West pointing the Athame straight ahead vibrate the words Morior Mori Mortuus Sum (Die, Expire, Pass, Die, Wither, A way Out, Fail, Decay)

9. Facing the North pointing the Athame straight ahead and vibrate the words Pereo Perire Perivi Peritus (Die, Pass Away, Be Ruined, Destroyed, Waste)

T Shape Body Formation:

✴ In front of me stands Santa Muerte
✴ Behind me stands Qayin
✴ On the right of me stands Baron Samedi
✴ On the left side of me stands Hel

✦ Within me burns the Pentagram of Death

✦ In the column stands the six-rayed Death Star

THE MIDDLE PILLAR RITUAL

With the Lesser Banishing Ritual of the Pentagram done and learned, as well as your own personally created banishing ritual it is now time to learn the middle pillar. Now bear in mind these rituals are in this book to give you a taste of the traditional methods out there. I do not expect you to do these rituals forever or for them to become a part of your integral practice. They exist as a simple reference for you to create your own new rituals of from. Just as a template should be.

1. Standing, feet together, facing east, visualize a white sphere above the head and vibrate: EH HEH YEH.

2. Visualize light descending to form a sphere at the throat, and vibrate: YE HOH VOH E LOH HEEM.

3. Visualize light descending to form a sphere at the heart, and vibrate: YE HOH VOH EL OAH VE DA ATH.

4. Visualize light descending to form a sphere at the genitals, and vibrate: SHAH DAI EL CHAI.

5. Visualize light descending to form a sphere at the feet, and vibrate: AH DOH NAI HA AH RETZ.

6. Visualize and feel a current of light rising from the feet, entering the body at the base of the spine and continuing upwards to flower out at the crown of the head to descend light a shower of light to re-enter at the feet. Continue to circulate the light at least four times.

7. Repeat the Lesser Banishing Ritual of the Pentagram and then close with the Kabbalistic Cross.

8. As we did previously with the Lesser Banishing Ritual of the Pentagram, proceed to create your own version of this ritual based on your individual needs.

MODIFIED MIDDLE PILLAR RITUAL

Now unlike the previous example of a modified ritual I am going to provide my own personal middle pillar modification. In this ritual, it has been made a lot simpler and fits to my own current of Norse Magick and Shamanism.

This ritual starts off with first Harrowing; creating sacred space for this ritual. The harrowing ritual I use is called the hammer rite.

RITE OF THE HAMMER

This rite is similar to the wiccan casting circle but with slight differences. In this rite, you will not be using your own power but rather calling on the power of Mjölnir.

This rite should be done before any other ritual work and then deliberately taken down after said ritual work is completed. For example, if you were to create a power object or relic such as a talisman or amulet you would do this rite, cast the circle, then you would do the relic work and then afterward take the hammer down to finish off.

For this ritual, you will need your ritual Mjölnir. If you don't have your hammer with you, you can instead use your fist however the actual ritual tool is preferred. Before starting the ritual make sure you are standing facing north (North is the direction of both Helheim and Asgard), unless the purpose of the ritual dictates otherwise starting at north is the default position.

PERFORMING THE RITE OF THE HAMMER

1. Face North and hold up your ritual Mjölnir or first. Hold it slightly in front of your head. Make the hammer sign (an inverted capital T) by bringing your first down in a straight line until it's in front of your waist, then move it from the left to the right of your body. Whilst you are doing this say:

    Hammer in the North, hallow and hold this sacred stead.

2. Once you have done this visualize a blue spot appearing just in front of your waist. Move clockwise to the east of the area you want to protect. Repeat the hammer sign and say:

    Hammer in the East, hallow and hold this sacred stead.

3. Visualize the spot becoming a line which runs in a quarter circle from north to east. Move clockwise to the South, repeat hammer sign and say:

    Hammer in the South, hallow and hold this sacred stead.

4. The line extends to a half circle in the south, move clock-wise to the west. Repeat hammer sign and say:

    Hammer in the West, hallow and hold this sacred stead.

5. Visualize the line becoming a complete circle around you at about waist height. Move to the center of the area, do the hammer sign above you and say:

    Hammer over me, hallow and hold this sacred stead.

6. The line becomes a dome above you. Face the ground do the hammer sign below your waist and say:

    Hammer under me, hallow and hold this sacred stead.

7. The dome becomes a complete Sphere extending into the ground below you. Move your fist over your heart and say:

In me, Midguard and Asgard.

8. From this point on you complete any ritual work you need to do and then proceed to take down the hammer. To take down the hammer you start below you and moving around anticlockwise. It will go from below, to above, west, south, east, and then north. At each direction saying:

Hammer thank you for holding this sacred stead.

9. As you do this visualize the sphere slowly coming undone at each point until it eventually disappears.

My Middle Pillar & Grounding Method

My method of the middle pillar has an addition to it. While most middle pillars do have a natural grounding in it I have deliberately included it in my own ritual. This rite for me both brings me back to center and balance as well as at the same time grounding my own energies to give an even bigger emphasis on balance.

While this practice isn't found in the Northern lore and has no basis in my ancestors practice this technique none the less has been adapted to my path as a Vitki and most importantly of all gets me results. The whole purpose of this technique is to balance out your energies and ground yourself back down to center, as well as acting as a middle pillar rite. Throughout our day to day life we pick up things most unknowingly that we can struggle to get rid of. Certain pains, negativity, and other various energies that we should make the habit of clearing out.

1. Find a place outside to do this grounding. You can do this in your back yard or deep in the forest if you like the main thing is to be outdoors. Preferable not on concrete but use what you have.

2. Take your shoes or boots of and put your feet together. Back straight, mouth closed and tongue pressed to the top of your mouth just behind the teeth with arms at your sides. Just stand like this for a few minutes and let your feet just naturally connect to the earth.

3. Once you feel ready, close your eyes, and begin to visualize yourself as a tree. Visualize roots beginning to grow out of the bottom of your feet and start to penetrate the earth. Slowly let the roots continue to grow until they are deep into the ground below you.

4. Spend a few minutes exploring your own body, and any negativity in your body, any aches, pains, negative emotions, and push them mentally down towards your feet/roots. Ask Jörð to receive and transform those energies and push them out into the earth.

5. Once you have pushed all the negativity and excess energies out begin to feel the roots begin to grow even further down into the earth. At the same time visualize branches begin to grow from your upper body and reach toward the sky. The roots grow until you reach a source of energy deep within the earth. You should be able to feel this energy, tingling sensations in the legs and body are a good indication.

6. Draw some of this energy up through your roots, through your body, passing up the spine and feel it nourish and energize your body and cleansing it as it goes.

7. Continue to draw the energy up into your branches and at the tips the energy becomes drops of water and slowly drips back down to the earth. Continue to do this for a few minutes until you are ready, then visualize the roots and branches gently shrinking back down into your body.

8. Thank Jörð.

Again, I cannot stress enough these rituals must be tailored to your individual needs, regardless of tradition. It has to be in line with your own sub-conscious.

THE OTHER LAWS
Chapter 9

N OW that the fundamentals are mostly down its time to fill in the rest of the gaps with the rest of the Hermetic principles. At this point you will have the majority of the formula down and you will be armed with the secrets of magick many have not dared to try and explore. Now we explore the rest of the Master Key of Hermeticism.

THE LAW OF RHYTHM

The Law of Rhythm is the understanding that life itself has cycles and tides that. The Magician must be coordinated with these tides not just for polarity sake but for truly being one with the flow of reality and self. Just as the moon has its phases life itself has never ending cycles. Our oceans have tides, our earth has seasons, not to mention the cycles of the earth itself. There are natural currents of our world that magickally are useful. As the law of vibration states energies synchronize.

Our magick and our ritual work can be tied to the phases of the moon, the seasons, and many other natural cycles. In fact, in shamanic work this is a definite principle to abide by. Many traditions stick to this so closely that it is often considered to be a defining factor for shamanism itself and in this tradition, that is also true. There is a natural ebb and flow of energy that magick swings to and with. With

Waning currents, which would be dusk, waning moon, autumn and winter is the best times to do rituals for cleansing and banishing; typically, magick to push things out. Whereas the waxing currents such as, sunrise, waxing moon, spring, and summer is the best times to do ritual for bring things into your life. Not to forget that certain Gods, Spirits and Wights can be more potent at these times.

Adhering to this law is akin to formulating your magickal work to the tides and cycles of reality itself. Be it by the days, phases or seasons these natural currents will push your magick with less resistance making your work potentially more potent and with better impact. Additionally, the uses of the sun, moon, day, and night can be a great benefit to certain areas of our shamanic work such as connecting with certain wights, calling on certain gods and harmonizing the self with natural flowing currents.

In light of the previous principles we can apply these rhythms in our magickal work through either mental subscription or meta-belief. Having the confidence of natural ebb and flow can provide not only boosts for our magickal work but also provide us with a means to time each one of our rituals correctly and more efficiently.

Let's take a mundane example. A person gets paid on the last day of every month and the day of that payday things flow in. As the month goes forward it starts to wane out. Pay comes, then it gets spent to buy food and other needs (this the flowing in) as the month goes by money drains, food drains, resources drain and things go out until they come back. That natural flow could be used in what's called mundane magick or manifestation through raw intent. These small details define the great magicians from the adepts.

Just as the moon has its phases and the oceans have their tides even the most mundane of currents have this natural ebb and flow. It is the responsibility of the magician to not only acknowledge these details but to capitalize on them magickally.

THE LAW OF CAUSE & EFFECT

This law is the simple concept that everything we do and not just magickal has consequences. Ørlög and the Web of Wyrd in my own tradition are greatly involved with this law. As you begin to understand the web of Wyrd in Norse magick you come to understand more so that everything we do more so magickally doesn't just affect our own individual self but other around us. However, in the mundane sense this is the truth that every action and indeed through or emotion has an effect in some form of another. When we look to how we cast out our intentions some of what we manifest especially if it is physical things can be the loss of another person. In extreme cases this can be the cost of life itself however, most cases aren't that severe.

This principle embodies the fact that there is a cause for every effect, an effect from every cause. It explains that, "everything happens according to the natural law", that nothing ever "merely happens". There is no such thing as chance, that while there are various planes of cause and effect, the higher dominating the lower planes, still nothing ever entirely escapes the law. Magick itself is a result of cause and effect and life itself is magick. Thus, any experience we have is a synchronicity of magick. While we can indeed bend the laws of magick we cannot escape them any more than we can exit the universe.

For this very reason, the magician should take care in everything that he/she does, choosing his or her actions wisely. Calculating ever move with surgical precision is the mark of great magician and in many ways a great shaman. With any magickal work first thinking about the consequences of that magick can save a lot of unwanted feedback at the end. It is said that a very small stone thrown into a pond can create very large ripples and even the smallest of our actions can cause great waves on the web of reality and I tend to agree with this statement.

THE LAW OF GENDER

All magick is symbolic of sex and this principle ties up the rest into understanding how magick works. Just as everything is duel we contain masculine and feminine forces as does everything else. While this law is similar to the law of polarity and does tie in with it, it does have key differences. All Magick is symbolic of sex. The conscious mind which is our masculine penetrating force, impresses our magick/intentions (thoughts, actions, words etc.) upon the feminine subconscious mind which then manifests a desired result. That result will appear in a synchronistic event in our life. All magick uses both a masculine force and a feminine and every work of magick is the work of birthing result and creation. Going back to polarity it is necessary for us to embrace both and maintain a balance.

It is from this law that I believe literal sex and magick have become well connected. Sex itself is an act of magick in the mundane sense and by looking at the process of creation we can see how magick mirrors this. It is also the understanding that while we can create beings physically we also have the ability to do it spiritually and magickally also. The sexual energy that we can produce can be utilized in many areas of magick, acting somewhat as a fuel. Many sexual related acts and practices can be used and the energy put off by that is often included in ritual work and spell casting.

THE PRINCIPLE OF CARE

This principle is not so much taken from Hermeticism itself nor is this principle usually written down but it is one of the underlying principles that to some degree encompasses the rest of the laws. The principle of care is simply just care. The magician in this case must care about what he/she is doing to have their magick work effectively. Thus, hitting back on the Law of Thelema. This means putting effort, time, and energy into the magickal work that he/she is doing.

It is often said that the more work you do on something the more energy you are putting into it magickally and I agree with this to an extent. It is not so much doing more work on something as doing too much can lead to unnecessary time being wasted but putting effort, care and most of all attention to detail into your work will pay off in the long run.

This principle of care however does have somewhat of a downside. Care can often end up becoming desperation and when magick is performed with desperation at its back it is must more difficult for that person to take their mind of the magick. One important concept to the act of intentional magick is to be able to set your intention and then forget about it. He who is certain of the result doesn't think twice about what he did. When performing magick you have to be able to shut your conscious mind out of the way as soon as you have done your casting. The sub-conscious will no manifest your result until the conscious mind is out of the way. When we are desperate we worry constantly about what we did and thus we can not only make our situation worse but we can hold back out magick and obscure our manifested result. The result of this is manifesting very little of what you actually wanted.

THE TWO PILLARS OF MAGICK

In my time of study and practice I have formed a small guideline on magick that seems to fit perfectly. A small conclusion to encompass this formula. While this two pillar system does not go into detail as this entire book has it does simply outline a simple truth about the formula of magick.

This is the two-pillar system for understanding magick at the mundane level. The first pillar is magick itself. All magick is the same machine, the psychological work of natural energies manifesting through our will and our sub-conscious. The principles we have just gone over are the mechanics for how all magick works regardless of tradition. The second pillar is symbolism and even this relates back to psychology.

Magick in every tradition bar its only really differs with its symbolism. The reason one path fits one individual and not another is because of how the relate to the symbolism. With any path the results you get are based upon your sub-conscious associations with the magickal symbols themselves. This is the one thing many practitioners of magick will not tell you. With any tradition or any ritual ask yourself with every symbol, what does this symbol mean to me? Not what does it mean, what does it mean to you?

By understanding what associations, you place on things will make you understand how to use them in magick. Be your own psychologist. What do I immediately thing when I see red, or a skull, or smell this type of incense. This is not just for magickal symbols but for anything. A man in a suit, a wasp a black cat, etc. Every object, sound, smell, and feeling is a symbol and so by understanding how your sub-conscious associates that symbol will make it useful in your ritual work. If you do a ritual for money use anything that you associate with that. It is because of this second pillar that magick is individual. Even with the same stimuli two people can have a different association. You need to understand your own mind and its associations. Know thyself, this is what that quote really means. It doesn't mean just know who you are, it means know your mind.

CLOSING

Chapter 10

ALL in all, this will have been a lot of information to take in. For myself in learning all this information it has taken me fifteen years to fully put this formula down for others to see. The work you have just gone through is the entire foundation of all my magickal work. In truth, it is my life's work. While I may be a Norse Vitki (Sorcerer & Shaman) the information laid out in this text is the core of which all of that sits upon.

Your mind at this point will most likely be exhausted. There is not only a lot of information to absorb but also many applications for you to implement along the way. My aim in this is to give you these insights so you can truly delve deeper into your own path to manifest the change and desires you wish. To not have to spend decades of your life trying to find the formula that sits in plain sight in front of us all.

This book is created with the intent of demystifying the occult and providing real insight and understanding on what exactly it is we are doing. It has been said by many that magick is a science we are yet to understand. I say they are wrong, they just have not looked close enough at the formula. This here is the science of magick and I hope that you will continue to be inspired by it, to create more rituals from it, and to hit the deepest depths you can with your pathworking.

Remember one key thing of all, your individual is more important than any collective tradition, and with your own self, you will do great things.

Stay True & Stay Awesome.

ASBJÖRN TORVOL

About the Author

My name is Asbjörn Torvol and I classify myself as a Norse Vitki (Sorcerer/Shaman). My history goes back quite a long way. From a very early age I was curious about the world of religion, philosophy, and spirituality. My curiosity lead me to search for new information and question the truths of many faiths. In my early teens, I discovered Paganism and Magick and my practice as a magician started. I experimented in Western Ceremonial Magick, Hermeticism, Thelema, and varying areas of psychological magick. In my late teens, I delved into necromancy with a deep fascination for the dead and the study of death itself. I found my true calling in Asatru/Heathenry and Norse Shamanism. After an intense awakening and calling to Thor I did not hesitate in beginning my research and practice.

I FOUND MY HOME IN NORSE MAGICK

After a lot of research and learning I decided that I wanted to learn Norse magick and truly commit to the path as a Vitki. It was at this same time I was taken as an apprentice Vitki by Dean Kirkland, who opened many doors of opportunity for me. All my life I have felt like a puzzle piece that doesn't fit anywhere but in the Norse Magick I found where I was meant to be. My goal in magick is to help others, share my knowledge and continue to progress myself. I wish to pass on the traditions and techniques that were passed down to me, and to continue to develop my own new spin on those same practices.

I VIEW THE GODS AS AN EXTENSION OF OURSELVES

Unlike many on my path I do not hold the belief that magick is exclusive nor is it special. Magick is very mundane at its core and the only difference between the magician/practitioner and everyone else is that the magician does it intentionally. Magick to me is not mystical but rather psychological. I have said many time magick is simply the mind. The work of the magician and indeed all magick is psychological in nature, and the inclusion of ritual tools and ingredients are to aid in the immersion of the psychological mind or as it is more commonly called psychodrama. In this same way, I do not believe my gods are entirely psychological but rather they are natural outward expressions as well as personifications of the self we are able to surface.

Norse Magick Taps into The Strongest Forces

In all of my magickal work I aim to include some element of science. Science has often been put at war against spirituality and I personally think this is a mistake. There is much of science that can aid in the work of the magician. I like to call this Scientific Spiritualism. Magick itself is psychological to me in nature and so including science is not just a way to understand the concepts of magick but also to aid in receiving more consistent results. However, excluding the science and psychology aspect my work as a Vitki takes me into the depths of nature. The biggest part of my path is connecting with natural currents and cycles in the attempt to become one with the natural web of reality. In this way, I am not limited in my magickal work by any societal chain as like the earth itself, I utilize both the great creation and devastating destruction.

BECOME A LIVING GOD
About the Publisher

B ECOME A Living God specializes in human ascent through the infinite power of black magick and most ingenious philosophy of the Left Hand Path. As a living force, BALG helps human magicians to smash the shackles of ideological slavery in order to awaken the true God and Goddess inside every man and woman.

View a complete catalog of unprecedented magick grimoires, spellbooks, pathworking courses, live rituals, talismans, and consultations at BecomeALivingGod.com/Catalog.

Made in the USA
Middletown, DE
21 June 2021